TO KILL A MOCKINGBIRD

Threatening Boundaries

TWAYNE'S MASTERWORK STUDIES

Robert Lecker, General Editor

TO KILL A MOCKINGBIRD

Threatening Boundaries

Claudia Durst Johnson

TWAYNE PUBLISHERS
An Imprint of Simon & Schuster Macmillan
New York

Prentice Hall International
London Mexico City New Delhi Singapore Sydney Toronto

Twayne's Masterwork Studies No. 139

To Kill a Mockingbird: Threatening Boundaries
Claudia Durst Johnson

Copyright © 1994 by Twayne Publishers

An Imprint of Simon & Schuster Macmillan
All rights reserved. No part of this book may be reproduced or transmitted in any form
or by any means, electronic or mechanical, including photocopying, recording, or by
any information storage and retrieval system, without permission in writing from the
Publisher.

An Imprint of Simon & Schuster Macmillan
1633 Broadway, New York, N.Y. 10019-6785

Library of Congress Cataloging-in Publication Data
Johnson, Claudia D.
   To kill a mockingbird: threatening boundaries / Claudia Durst Johnson
      p.   cm — (Twaynes's masterwork studies; no. 139)
   Includes bibliographical references (p.) and index.
   ISBN 0-8057-8068-8—ISBN 0-8057-8113-7 (pbk).
   1. Lee, Harper. To kill a mockingbird. I. Title. II. Series.
PS3562.E353T634 1994
813'.54—dc20   93-42829
                                                                          CIP

The paper used in this publication meets the minimum requirements of American
National Standard for Information Services—Permanence of Paper for Printed Library
Materials. ANSI Z3948-1984. ∞ ™
                                  ◯
10 9 8 7 6 5 4 3 2 1 (hc)
10 9 8 7 6 5   (pb)

Printed in the United States of America

For
Vernon, Catherine and Lillian

Contents

Nelle Harper Lee. *Reprinted with permission of the University of Alabama Alumni Publications.*

Note on the References and Acknowledgments

I would like to thank HarperCollins Publishers for permission to quote extensively from *To Kill a Mockingbird*.

A similar version of the section on legal boundaries appeared in *Studies in American Fiction* (Autumn 1991) as an article entitled "The Secret Courts of Men's Hearts: Code and Law in Harper Lee's *To Kill a Mockingbird*." I am indebted to the journal for allowing me permission to include an altered version here.

I also appreciate the permission of the University of Alabama Alumni Publications to reproduce the photograph of Nelle Harper Lee that appears as the frontispiece of this volume. The photograph was widely used when reviews of *To Kill a Mockingbird* first appeared in the press.

Several friends and colleagues assisted me in this endeavor: From the project's inception, Bruce Kupelnick gave me encouragement, advice, and the benefit of his wide reading. Professor James B. McMillan was generous with his knowledge of Harper Lee's history, especially her days at the University of Alabama, where, as distinguished linguist and director of the University of Alabama Press, he served as one of her mentors. Yueng Hwa Bae spent many tedious hours tracking down references and checking details, as well as suggesting productive avenues for investigation that had not before occurred to me, and research librarians Larry Harbin and David Lowe saved me many hours of work by taking their own valuable time to help me ferret out the publication history of *To Kill a Mockingbird*. David steered me to the important legal commentary on the work that

I would have overlooked without his help. Professor Beth Burch generously provided me with materials on the censorship of the novel, and the history of the book's use in secondary schools. Of special assistance was Larry Watts, poet and historian, who is an astute and loving student of Alabama, the state of his birth.

Most of all, I'd like to thank Nelle Harper Lee for writing *To Kill a Mockingbird*, a work that really has made a difference, and for graciously agreeing to spend an afternoon talking with me about the history of the novel.

Chronology:
Nelle Harper Lee's Life and Times

1880	Amasa Coleman Lee born in rural Butler County, Alabama, on 19 July.
1913	Moves to Monroeville, Alabama, and is admitted to the bar in 1915.
1926	Nelle Harper Lee is born on 28 April in Monroeville to Amasa Coleman and Frances Finch Lee.
1927–1939	Amasa Lee serves in the Alabama State Legislature.
1929–1947	Edits the *Monroe Journal*.
1928–1933	Truman Capote, a childhood friend of Harper Lee's, lives with relatives in Monroeville, next door to the Lee family.
1931	Scottsboro Incident occurs in March and begins litigation that will continue for twenty years.
1932	U.S. Supreme Court reverses the Scottsboro conviction and orders a new trial. Scottsboro youths retried.
1933	Judge Horton rejects jury's finding of guilty and subsequently fails to be reelected.
1936	Another retrial of Scottsboro case.
1937	All major Alabama newspapers urge the release of the Scottsboro defendants.
1944–1945	Harper Lee attends Huntingdon College, a private school for women in Montgomery, Alabama.
1945–1950	Continues her undergraduate studies at the University of Alabama, where she writes for several student publications and in 1946–47 edits the *Rammer-Jammer*, a humor magazine. To the October issue she contributes a one-act play satirizing a

southern politician who proclaims that "Our very lives are being threatened by the hordes of evildoers full of sin. . . .SIN, my friends. . .who want to tear down all barriers of any kind between ourselves and our colored friends," and who argues in favor of creating stricter voting requirements based, ironically, on the ability to interpret the constitution (an actual requirement for would-be voters in Alabama at the time). In the February issue she parodies country newspapers. One such is *The Jackassonian Democrat*, complete with the logo of two white-sheeted figures carrying burning crosses.

1947   Enrolls in the University of Alabama School of Law to have stack privileges in the library. Her education includes a term as an exchange student at Oxford University in England.

1948   Capote publishes his first novel, *Other Voices, Other Rooms*; one of the novel's characters, the tomboyish Idabel, is based in part on Lee.

1950   Lee moves to New York City, where she works as an airline reservation clerk for Eastern Air Lines and British Overseas Airways Corporation. Several years later Lee quits her job when she receives a loan from friends to write full time for a year.

The last of the Scottsboro boys is paroled.

1955   Rosa Parks is arrested on 1 December for violating the bus segregation ordinance in Montgomery. Four days later the famous bus boycott commences in that city.

1955–1956   A black woman, Autherine Lucy, attempts to enroll in the University of Alabama as a student, and eventually, following months of litigation, is forced to withdraw after mobs of whites begin rioting on the campus.

1956   The bus boycott ends on 21 December and buses are integrated.

1958   Harper Lee completes the first draft of *To Kill a Mockingbird* (*TKM*) in June and delivers the manuscript to editor Tay Hohoff at J. B. Lippincott. Lee begins the final editing process.

1959   The report of the murder of the Clutter family of Kansas appears in the *New York Times* on 15 November, catching the attention of Capote, who asks Lee to accompany him to Kansas to research a book on the case. By this time, *TKM* is entirely complete and in press. In December, Lee and Capote travel to Garden City, Kansas, where interviews of townspeople proceed. The two writers both make mental notes on each interview, returning at nights to the Warren Hotel to type the day's information. Capote, in an interview with George

Plimpton in the *New York Times Book Review*, details some of Lee's assistance on the novel: "She went on a number of interviews; she typed her own notes, and I had these and could refer to them. She was extremely helpful in the beginning, when we weren't making much headway with the town's people, by making friends with the wives of the people I wanted to meet." Of his friend, Capote said, "She is a gifted woman, courageous, and with a warmth that instantly kindles most people, however suspicious or dour" (January 16, 1966). Lee is dining with Capote at the chief detective's house on the night the suspects are arrested.

1960   Lee and Capote are present for the opening of the Clutter case trial on 22 March. This is one of many trips on which Lee accompanies Capote to Kansas, giving him encouragement when the investigation becomes discouraging. In July, official publication date of *TKM*, issued by J. B. Lippincott, is delayed until fall, when several book clubs choose it as a selection; it becomes a Literary Guild Selection, a Book-of-the Month Club Alternate, and a Readers Digest Condensed Book. *TKM* becomes a British Book Society Choice and is subsequently issued in the United Kingdom by Heinemann.

1961   *TKM* wins the Alabama Association Award in April. Lee also writes an article entitled "Love—in Other Words," which is printed in the April issue of *Vogue*. In the spring, Robert Mulligan and Alan Pakula purchase the film rights to *TKM*, which Pakula produces and Mulligan directs for Universal Pictures. Gregory Peck is chosen for the part of Atticus Finch. Harper Lee declines an offer to write the screenplay; the task falls to Horton Foote. *TKM* wins the Pulitzer Prize for Literature in April. Harper Lee is the first woman to win the prize since Ellen Glasgow received it in 1942. By this time, the novel has sold five hundred thousand copies and has been translated into ten languages. In December, the novel wins the Brotherhood Award of the National Conference on Christians and Jews. Also, Lee's "Christmas to Me" appears in *McCall's*. The story is an account of opening a card given to her by friends on Christmas morning: "You have one year off from your job to write whatever you please. Merry Christmas." (Lee actually declined the money as a gift but accepted it as a loan, which she paid back with interest.)

1962   Wins the Bestseller's Paperback Award for the year. Two years after the publication of *TKM*, it has sold two and a half million copies in hardback editions and two million paperback copies.

In May, Lee receives an honorary doctorate from Mount Holyoke College. She also goes to Hollywood as a special consultant to producers of the film based on her novel. The film, *To Kill a Mockingbird*, premieres, and that winter is nominated for eight Academy Awards, ultimately winning four, including best actor (Peck) and best screenplay (Foote). Peck pays tribute to Lee, displaying Amasa Lee's gold watch, which she had given the actor.

1963   In April, Capote and Lee travel from Monroeville to Kansas, where the murderers of the Clutter family are on death row. Just hours before his execution, killer Perry Smith writes a letter to Capote and Lee.

1964   Publication of Horton Foote's film script of *TKM* with foreword by Harper Lee.

1965   Random House publishes Capote's *In Cold Blood*. The dedication reads: "For Jack Dunphy and Harper Lee, with my love and gratitude."

1966   Lee is appointed to National Council on the Arts by President Lyndon Baines Johnson. She scouts for a fitting place for the filming of Capote's "A Christmas Memory."

1969   Publication of Christopher Sergel's play based on Harper Lee's novel. The play meets with long-standing success in stock companies in the United States and becomes extremely popular in England in the 1980s. It is still a standard in provincial theaters in both countries.

1974   The Popular Library books publishes its 94th printing of *TKM*.

1977   Publication of *TKM* in a special limited edition by Franklin Publications.

1982   Publication of *TKM* in a special limited edition by *Southern Living* magazine.

1990   Lee receives an honorary doctorate from the University of Alabama.

1991   A highly praised television series, "I'll Fly Away," set in the 1950s South, is about a small-town lawyer who frequently tries cases involving race, and rears his three children with the help of a black housekeeper, rather than a wife.

LITERARY AND HISTORICAL CONTEXT

1

Racial Climate in the Deep South

The historical context of *To Kill a Mockingbird*[1] is formed by the national economic depression of the 1930s and the regional history of race relations in the South, as exemplified by the notorious Scottsboro trial, whose setting was very like that of the novel—Alabama in the 1930s. Of significance, as well, is the drama of racial change played out largely in Alabama in the 1950s, as Harper Lee was writing the novel, and as it made its appearance on the national scene. That drama specifically involves the defiant gesture of Mrs. Rosa Parks and of the Montgomery bus boycott undertaken in the face of ugly opposition; the attempt of Autherine Lucy to enroll at the University of Alabama in Tuscaloosa; and the violent beginning of the end of segregation in the deep South.

RACIAL TENSION DURING THE DEPRESSION

The setting of *TKM* is the supposed end of the Great Depression, which had hit the rural South particularly hard. Even though, as historian Wayne Flynt argues, the rural poor—like the residents of Old

3

Sarum in the novel—saw the depression as just another episode in a life of abject poverty,[2] the most afflicted were, as George Brown Tindall writes, the farmers, "the very group that had shared least in the decade's prosperity." [3] Pulled down along with King Cotton were the banks and entire economies of the small towns in the rural South—cotton-growing areas, like the real Monroeville and the fictional Maycomb. "In 1932," Tindall writes, "farm incomes fell to 39 percent of the 1929 level and receipts from cotton alone to 31 percent; both far outdistanced the general decline of incomes to 58 percent" (Tindall, 354). What is outside the scope of the novel, but which nevertheless affected the racial and class dynamics of the state, eventually leading to both violence and reform, were the unemployment and poverty in the industrial and mining areas of northern Alabama, where Communist and other radical union organizers posed a threat to the entrenched power base.

Although in some instances poor whites and blacks joined together for the first time to better their lots, the desperate unpredictability of the economic situation, competition for jobs, and long-standing racial fear reinforced bigotry. W. J. Cash in *The Mind of the South* (1969) contends that World War I, rather than enlarging the field of tolerance of the southerner who had come into contact with nationalities and cultures so unlike his own, instead increased his sense of superiority and fear, returning him to the South more intolerant of difference than he had ever been before. Many southerners reacted violently to the multiple threats to order and meaning that they perceived, whether those threats were economic collapse, unionism, Communism, Rooseveltism, or a breakdown of the class and, especially, racial boundaries that defined their society. The vehemence with which these traditional boundaries were maintained is at the center of Lee's novel. It is also at the center of America's single most significant legal case involving race relations, one that exploded in the public press in the 1930s. In looking at the historical context of *TKM*, it is essential to examine that case—the notorious Scottsboro trial. Legal historians, like Thomas Shaffer and Timothy Hall, who are familiar with *TKM*, invariably are struck by the similarities between the fictional trial of Tom Robinson and the actual Scottsboro case. The most conspicuous parallels are the commonality of time and place. Both trials occurred in the state of Alabama in the 1930s. Both arose from charges of interracial rape. Yet the parallels go much deeper.

The Scottsboro incident occurred on 25 March 1931, when nine black youths were arrested as they disembarked the cars of a freight train in a little town called Paint Rock in northern Alabama. They were charged with raping two white women who were also riding the cars on the train. Although the case was not settled until 1976, the major trials occurred in 1931, with mistrials and appeals in 1933 and 1936, during which years the case was meticulously covered and commented upon by every newspaper in the state of Alabama and every major paper outside the state. The parallels between the trials of Tom Robinson, the black man in Lee's novel, and the Scottsboro youths underscore a pattern of attitudes in the South. That societal pattern sets up a foundation from which to explore one of the most important conflicts in the novel—the one between Atticus Finch, who defends Tom Robinson, and the community of Maycomb, Alabama, where Tom and Atticus live and where the trial takes place. The central parallels between the trial in the novel and the Scottsboro trial are three: the threat of lynching; the issue of a southern jury's composition; and the intricate symbolic complications arising from the interweave of race and class when a lower-class white woman wrongfully accuses a black man or men. The centrality of the woman's testimony, her behavior on the witness stand, the cover-up of another crime or secret, and the important issue of her low social standing in the Scottsboro case correspond to the situation constructed by Lee in *TKM*.

Note first the shadow of lynching that menaces the accused in both the real trial and the novel's. The threat of Tom Robinson's being lynched occurs in the novel when, after he is transferred to the city jail, a crowd of townspeople visits Atticus at his house at night, and, later, when a mob from the community called Old Sarum drives into town to ask Atticus to move from in front of the jail (that he wisely decided to guard) so that they can abduct Tom. These incidents are well within the realm of plausibility in the South during the thirties. As Virginia Hamilton writes in her history of Alabama, lynching had become a way of life in the South, and in Alabama alone between the years 1889 and

1940, there are 303 documented lynchings, almost entirely of black people.[4] Writes historian Dan T. Carter, quoting from the Southern Commission on the Study of Lynching, "From 1900 to 1930, the number of lynchings gradually decreased from more than a hundred to less than a dozen annually. Beginning in 1930, however, the number rose to an average of almost twenty per year."[5] Outside the jail in Scottsboro, Alabama, a real scene, on a somewhat larger scale but very like the one in the novel, had occurred in 1931 after the arrest of the accused black youths. That night, writes Dan T. Carter in his history of the trials, "Farmers from the nearby hills began gathering, and by dusk a crowd of several hundred stood in front of the two-story jail." Most of those, like the Old Sarum mob, were poor white farmers (Carter, 7). In the wake of the Scottsboro incident itself there were two notorious cases of white men taking the lives of black men accused of rape. In neither case were the killers arrested. Another incident occurred in Birmingham in 1931, when a black man who was an invalid and clearly incapable of committing the crime of which he was accused, was shot by his accuser's brother. In another instance in 1933, three men accused of rape were simply taken out and shot rather than being brought to trial.

Also reminiscent of the Scottsboro trial was the fictional Maycomb county's jury composition, which derived from a selection process that included no blacks and no women, and which allowed businessmen and professional people to have themselves excused from jury duty for any reason. In every sense, it is the jury system, and hence, jury composition that dooms the innocent black man in the novel. In the same way, it was the defense's challenge to the jury system in Alabama that eventually allowed the release of the Scottsboro defendants. After losing the cases in the first rounds of his defense of several of his clients, Samuel Leibowitz, the famous defense attorney from New York, mounted a new defense based on the exclusion of African-Americans from jury lists in Alabama, a case that eventually went to the Supreme Court. In 1935 the Court found in favor of the Scottsboro youths. The history of the trials includes the testimony of Scottsboro's registrar and commissioner, who declared that no black person and no woman was capable of serving on a jury, supporting their contention with the declaration that, even though there were black people who were educated, held professional jobs, and had good reputations, none had "sound judgment" and "they will nearly all steal" (Carter, 195). Challenge to jury selection continued even after the Supreme Court decision, as Leibowitz proved that old jury lists had recently been tampered with, and that the names of some prominent black citizens had been added after the fact.

The most telling and destructive cultural peculiarity of the region underscored in the Scottsboro case, and also pertinent to Lee's narrative, is the symbolic clash between the dark-skinned, sexual male and the white-skinned female, who is assumed, by virtue of her gender and color, to be chaste, despite all evidence to the contrary. Both Mayella Ewell in Lee's novel and Victoria Price in the Scottsboro case complicate the attempt to uphold pure southern womanhood: Mayella, a lonely woman and the victim of incest, attempts to seduce the black man, Tom, while Victoria Price was commonly known to be a prostitute, and was afraid of being arrested on a morals charge. Indeed, Bob Ewell's coarsely worded description of the rape of his daughter, which elicits a warning from the judge in the case, is an echo of Victoria Price's grossly and graphically obscene description of her rape in words that might be expected—indeed were assumed by the defense— to be used only by a prostitute. Still, the symbolic force attached to these women as white, female accusers of black men was enough to counteract reality. Victoria Price had, ironically, become a symbol of the old South, and the accused black rapists and their defenders were actually thought of as assaulting "the South's entire social structure" (Carter, 278). "In 1932 the Winston-Salem, North Carolina *Journal* noted that 'in the South it has been tradition. . .that its white womanhood shall be held inviolate by an "inferior race."' And it mattered not whether the woman was a spotless virgin or a 'nymph de pave'" (Carter, 105). In the trials that occurred in the winter of 1933–34, Judge William W. Callahan underscored this attitude, for he would permit no testimony from the physicians who had examined Victoria Price after the alleged rape, an examination that would have established that she had not had intercourse, much less been raped in the hours during which the rapes were to have taken place. Neither would

Judge Callahan allow any testimony detailing Price's actions on the night before the rape, testimony that would have proved the defense's contention that she charged the black men with rape in an attempt to evade being arrested for violation of the Mann Act, that is, crossing state lines for immoral purposes. As New York's *Herald Tribune* reported, Price "might be a fallen woman, but by God she is a white woman" (Carter, 295).

In both the fictional Robinson trial and the real Scottsboro trial, the social class of the woman bringing the charges, as well as her lack of respectability, is at issue. As members of the poorer class, these women's actions were scarcely surprising in that, lacking the paternalism that upper- and upper-middle-class whites often adopted toward blacks, the poor white typically was extreme and often violent in his or her racial bigotry. At the same time, the class to which both Mayella Ewell and Victoria Price belonged complicates the attempt to establish them as symbols of southern womanhood. It also makes it impossible to deny them compassion. Mayella Ewell is, of course, a victim for whom the black man, Tom, has the audacity to feel pity. Similarly, Victoria Price, utterly despicable in so many ways, is a victim of a harsh caste system. As a woman who made a hard living occasionally working in the textile mills when she could find work during the depression, she told a reporter as the case began, "'Mister, I never had a "break" in my life'" (Carter, 14). Dan T. Carter sums up his own attitude toward her, after he participated in a trial in 1977 occasioned by Victoria Price's lawsuit against NBC on the grounds that the network had broadcast a libelous documentary based on Carter's book:

> As I watched her hobble from the courtroom, however, I was struck by my ambivalence toward this woman. During the 1930s she had struggled to survive on two to three dollars a week as a cotton mill worker. In the midst of this collapsing economy she had lived by her wits and (according to her accusers) the use of the only collateral she possessed, her body. . . .But if she had lied about the rape, she had done so because she lived in a setting which encouraged and rewarded this monstrous lie. (Carter, 462)

A comparison between Price and the abused Mayella, who takes loving care of her red geraniums, is easily drawn.

One of the most interesting parallels of the two trials is found in the fear and hatred that both lower-class, uneducated accusers feel in the presence of the defense attorneys—Atticus Finch in one case and Samuel Leibowitz in the other. Scout, Atticus's daughter, reports that "I never saw anybody glare at anyone with the hatred Mayella showed when she left the stand and walked by Atticus's table" (*TKM*, 188). Just so, "Mrs. Price looked at Leibowitz with such venom that one reporter thought for a moment she was going to strike her tormentor" (Carter, 212). The women's responses to their questioners would suggest that much more than their stories of rape is being challenged. It is as if their very souls are being threatened by these men who are so powerful and so different from them in social class, education, and intellect, as if the whole struggle of the proletariat is being waged between two individuals in a courtroom.

There are other echoes of the Scottsboro incident in *To Kill a Mockingbird*: for example, the collection taken up at Tom Robinson's church, which Scout observes, to assist the accused man and his family parallels a black Chattanooga minister's raising $50 for the defense of the Scottsboro defendants on the day of their arrests. And, historian Virginia Hamilton's description of the crowd attending the Scottsboro trial is strongly reminiscent of the festive mood of the white people from every walk of life streaming to the fictional trial of Tom Robinson, underscoring the holiday spirit with which a clan approaches the sacrifice of a scapegoat: "Poor-white farmers in faded overalls and women with babies on their hips jostled for seats in the courtroom or surged about the square awaiting what to them was the only conceivable verdict. These hill people, most of them illiterate, ill-nourished, and impoverished, possessed little of value save their white skin" (Hamilton, 89).

In Atticus's often-quoted address to the jury ("There is one way in this country in which all men are created equal—there is one human institution that makes a pauper the equal of a Rockefeller. . . .That institution, gentlemen, is a court" (205) is an echo of the 1933 address to the courtroom by Judge James E. Horton, one of the heroes of the

Scottsboro trial, in his attempt to forestall violence against the defendants and their attorney: "Now, gentlemen, under our law when it comes to the courts we know neither native nor alien, we know neither Jew nor Gentile, we know neither black nor white. . . .It is our duty to mete out even-handed justice" (Carter, 202).

The general attitude, even of more progressive members of the populace, is similar in both cases. After the first guilty verdict was rendered in the Scottsboro case and one of the local defense attorneys in this first trial in 1931, Milo Moody, turned to the business of helping the National Association for the Advancement of Colored People (NAACP) file appeals, he was severely criticized by one of his professional acquaintances, who declared that it was all well and good for Moody to try the case, but he was wrong to continue working on the case after the defendants had been sentenced to death (Carter, 179). In a similar fashion in *TKM*, the old courthouse hangers-on acknowledge Atticus's obligation to try the Robinson case as a court-appointed attorney, but criticize him for choosing to actually defend his client: "Yeah, but Atticus aims to defend him. That's what I don't like about it" (*TKM*, 163).

In both trials, the mode of addressing "inferiors" in the courtroom becomes a matter of peculiar magnitude. In the Scottsboro case, chief defense counsel Samuel Leibowitz astounded the southern courtroom by asking that one of his black clients be addressed as "Mr.," and by using that form of address himself. As Carter writes, "Leibowitz's insistence on referring to Negro witnesses as 'Mr.' had only perplexed the spectators" (Carter, 202). Address was also of consequence in the Scottsboro trial when Leibowitz, probably in an attempt to imply that the accuser's traveling companion was not her husband, asked, "Miss Price, shall I call you Miss Price or Mrs. Price?" At this question, one of the reporters noted that Victoria Price "looked at her interrogator as though he were a poisonous snake circling her chair" (Carter, 205). In a similar vein, in the trial in Maycomb, Mayella Ewell becomes enraged when Atticus calls her "Miss Mayella," because as a lower-class young woman, she has never been addressed with respect and thinks he is making fun of her.

A final parallel between the posttrial days of the novel and the Scottsboro trial: One of the convicted Scottsboro defendants, seemingly in an effort to escape from custody, is shot by a deputy; in the same way, Tom Robinson is shot repeatedly by prison guards when he attempts to climb the prison fence.

THE CLIMATE AT MID-CENTURY

Also of historical significance is the national climate in which *To Kill a Mockingbird* came to fruition—the social and political environment in which the novel made its debut, and the tremendous impact that environment had on the reception of the novel. The book was engendered at the height of the civil rights movement in the South. In 1954, at about the time that Harper Lee was beginning to devote full time to writing her novel, the first ruling of the *Brown v. Board of Education* Supreme Court decision, outlawing the maintenance of segregation in education, was being handed down. It was a decision that would propel the South into violent conflict and eventually lead to the legal desegregation of all public aspects of southern life. Historians see the real beginning of the end of segregation in the South as occurring on 1 December 1955, when Mrs. Rosa L. Parks was arrested in Montgomery, Alabama, for violating the bus segregation ordinance that forced blacks to sit in the back of the bus. On 5 December 1955, a boycott of the Montgomery bus system began under the leadership of the early civil rights activist Mr. E. D. Nixon, and, later, the Reverend Martin Luther King, Jr. One year later, on 21 December 1956, segregation of transportation in Montgomery ended. Step by step, other segregation ordinances throughout the South were challenged, but rarely ever without violence. Virginia Foster Durr, a civil rights activist from Montgomery, records the frequent bombings of black churches and homes of ministers in Montgomery in 1956 and 1957.[6]

In the spring of 1955, while Lee was writing the story of black and white relationships in Monroeville, Alabama, and the bus boycott was continuing in Montgomery, the nation's attention was drawn to another place in Alabama—Tuscaloosa, seat of the state university where Lee herself had attended school. Two black women, Pollie Ann Myers and Autherine Lucy, had their university admissions rescinded when it was discovered that they were black. After the women sued for admission and the university unsuccessfully appealed the court's ruling in favor of the women, the institution was forced to allow Autherine Lucy to enroll for the 1956 winter term. Myers withdrew under pressure.

Carl Grafton and Anne Permaloff, writing about the incident in *Big Mules and Branchheads: James E. Folson and Political Power in Alabama*, describe the scene on campus, which was reported as headline news throughout the nation:

> The university began to rumble like a volcano about to erupt. Crosses were burned, and motels and hotels began to fill with out-of-town and out-of-state visitors. . . .
>
> On Friday, Saturday and Sunday nights just before classes began white demonstrators numbering approximately one thousand snaked around the campus and into the street chanting "Keep, 'Bama white" and "Hey, hey, ho, ho, Autherine's got to go," throwing rocks and firecrackers, battering automobiles driven by blacks, and harassing President Oliver Carmichael at his home. Monday began the first full week of classes. It was a frightening, violent day for which university officials, city police, and the state highway patrol were almost completely unprepared, despite the three nights of violence. Mobs, at times numbering two thousand people, many unconnected with the university and encouraged by KKK and White Citizens' Council members, succeeded in driving Lucy from the campus.[7]

A full appreciation, not to mention understanding of *To Kill A Mockingbird* derives from a grasp of these events in Alabama in the 1930s and 1950s. Furthermore, it would be hardly rash to assume that the composition of *TKM* was in some way affected by the events of the 1930s and 1950s. And, it can be said unequivocally that the reception of *TKM* was profoundly affected by the events of the 1950s.

2

The Importance of *To Kill a Mockingbird*

To Kill a Mockingbird is one of those books that has reached large numbers of readers and has made a significant difference in the lives of individuals and the culture as a whole. One year after its publication in 1960, it had gone through 500,000 copies and had been translated into ten languages. The novel's exceptional popularity can be seen in the fact that Popular Library, which began publishing *TKM* in paperback in 1962, by 1974 had issued 94 printings. In a study of best-sellers, Alice P. Hackett and James H. Burke found that in an 80-year period, from 1895 to 1975, *TKM* was the seventh best-selling book in the nation, and the third best-selling novel. By 1975, 11,113,909 copies of the book had been sold, and by 1982, over 15,000,000.[1] Over the years the novel has been published by numerous other presses, sometimes changing publishers as publishing houses were bought by different corporations, or combined. *TKM* bears the imprint of Reader's Digest, Heinemann, Harper and Row, HarperCollins, Lippincott, Ulverscroft, Warner, Fawcett, Popular Library, Penguin, Feltrinelli, McClelland, Vaovao, Franklin, Kurashino, Southern Living, Planeta Lenizdat, Plaza and Jan'es, Minerva, Buccaneer, G.K. Hall, and Longman, among others. *Books in Print* and the On-Line

Catalog of the Library of Congress indicate that since 1960 *TKM* has never been out of print in either hardcover or paperback, and remains popular in languages other than English.

One mark of the widespread exposure of the book is that since its publication in 1960, the novel has appeared on secondary school reading lists as often as any book in English. Arthur Applebee in *A Study of Book-Length Works Taught in High School English Courses* find that *TKM* has been consistently one of the ten most frequently required books in secondary schools since its publication in 1960.[2] A 1990 survey of junior high and high school English teachers and librarians indicates that *TKM* is the fourth most frequently required book in secondary schools.[3] A measure of the frequency with which students have been exposed to the book is the number of teachers' guides it has spawned—some 20 different editions of reading and study guides over a period of 33 years.

A sign of the novel's impact on the people who read it is found in a "Survey of Lifetime Reading Habits," conducted in 1991 by the Book-of-the-Month Club and the Library of Congress's Center for the Book. The survey found that among the books mentioned by its 5,000 respondents, Harper Lee's *TKM* was second only to the Bible in being "most often cited as making a difference" in people's lives.[4]

Censorship of the Novel

The importance of the novel cannot be separated from the controversy that it has elicited. *TKM* has a secure place in the history of books that have been challenged by parents or various watchdog organizations. The banning of *TKM* has been the subject of an article by Jill P. May, who argues that the work is a "case study of how such censorship works in young adult literature."[5] Amazingly, the novel is among the 30 books most frequently challenged since 1965. A study of book censorship efforts in schools and libraries includes a list of 25 objections regarding book content that English teachers and librarians most often hear about books on their shelves and reading lists. At least ten of these objections have been raised about *TKM*, and include: the portrayal of conflict between children and their elders, or children questioning the wisdom of their elders; profanity or questionable language; ungrammatical speech by characters; use of black dialect; references to the supernatural or witchcraft; depictions of violence; references to sex; negative statements about persons in authority, the United States, or American traditions; the lack of portrayal of the family unit as the basis of American life; and unfavorable presentations of blacks.[6] The novel has been challenged equally by the political left and right from California to Virginia. May finds a peculiar and ironic pattern in the censorship of the novel. In the mid-sixties, after *TKM* had become a standard work in junior high and high school curricula, the complaints came from southern conservatives. Although, May argues, the stated objections were to profanity, sex scenes, and immorality, in such cases the underlying reason betrays itself to be the "candid portrayal of Southern white attitudes" (May, 91). A few lawsuits were launched, but no legal action ever came to pass. Instead, May writes, those who brought objections hoped that the mere label of "immorality" would stick to the book and serve to remove it from reading lists. What May calls the second round of objections, in the seventies and early eighties, took place in the East and Midwest by the religious right and African-Americans, with the latter group objecting to *TKM*'s condonation of institutional racism.

The immense importance of the novel has emerged in large part because of its impact on stereotyping. The issue is obviously not a simple one, because some commentators, even friendly ones, have seen some degree of stereotyping in the novel's situation and characters, especially of the novel's blacks and poor whites. Historian Wayne Flynt, for example, in *Poor But Proud*, his history of poor whites in Alabama, cites *TKM* as an example of fiction giving "poor whites no respite." While he admires the courage of the work, in his judgment Lee "relied on familiar stereotypes" of the kindly black victim, the courageous white lawyer, and the villainous white trash (Flynt, 214, 215). But the courageous southern lawyer was a rarity at the time of this novel's publication, and has become a type only since then. In fact, at the time, Lee's portrayal of this character disturbed the

North's stereotypes of southerners. The impossible romanticism of Margaret Mitchell's characters in *Gone with the Wind*, the primitive animality of Erskine Caldwell's characters in *Tobacco Road*, and the jaded degeneracy of William Faulkner's characters in *Absalom, Absalom!*, not to mention the much-publicized racism of the mob that threatened Autherine Lucy, were all moderated by the civilized, highly educated, morally courageous Atticus Finch. An early reviewer for the *New York Times*, Frank H. Lyell, draws attention, just after the novel's publication, to the fact that "Miss Lee has not tried to satisfy the current lust for morbid, grotesque tales of Southern depravity."[7] And another critic, writing for *Commonweal*, notes, "What a greenhorn from the North may enjoy most is how quietly and completely he is introduced to ways of seeing and feeling and acting in the Deep South."[8]

Moreover, *TKM*'s importance arises from its challenge of the southerner's stereotype of African-Americans. In a *New Yorker* article of October 1992, some 32 years after the publication of *TKM*, James Carville, Bill Clinton's presidential campaign manager, is described by historian Gary Wills as spending his formative years in the 1960s South: "It was then also that he read what he calls the most important book in his life, Harper Lee's *To Kill a Mockingbird*. 'I just knew, the minute I read it, that she was right and I had been wrong'—about blacks. 'I don't want to make it noble, or anything. I was just bored with all the talk of race.'"[9]

Black stereotypes there may well be in the novel, but there is also a black housekeeper who has learned to read and has taught her son to read from legal commentaries. There is also a black man who can feel pity for a white woman who has accused him of raping her. These are not the typical portraits of African-Americans that white southerners held at the time.

There are, also, at times stripped of rationalizations and sometimes parodying long-standing acculturation, the naive views of children toward what William Faulkner called the "dispossessed" in southern society, and toward the entrenched system that kept them victimized. The children hold up a mirror to hypocrisy, and many southerners, like James Carville, acknowledged seeing themselves in that mirror.

THE LEGAL CONTROVERSY

The most ardent testimony to the continuing importance of *TKM* comes not from students of literature, but from students of the law. Many attorneys have asserted that Atticus Finch has been a hero and a model for them on a very personal plain. Indeed, Atticus Finch seems to have resurfaced in the consciousness of lawyers in the face of attacks on the profession for its callousness and greediness in the late eighties and early nineties. Finch is described by David Margolick, legal writer for the *New York Times*, as a man "who taught a community and his two young children about justice, decency and tolerance, and who drove a generation of real-life Jems and Scouts to become lawyers themselves."[10] Claudia Carter, California attorney and onetime president of the Barristers, a society of young lawyers within the California bar association, is fairly typical in her argument that lawyers should turn to Atticus in marshaling arguments in defense of their profession. Writing in a short article entitled "Lawyers as Heroes: The Compassionate Activism of a Fictional Attorney Is a Model We Can Emulate" in the *Los Angeles Lawyer* in 1988, she contends that it is Atticus's compassion, responsibility to others, and gentleness outside the courtroom that have made him a hero to young lawyers: "I had lots of heroes when I was growing up. Some were men, some were women; some were real and some were imaginary people in books I read. Only one remains very much 'alive' for me. He is a character in Harper Lee's novel *To Kill a Mockingbird*. . . .Atticus made me believe in lawyer-heroes."[11] Another testimonial comes from a trial lawyer, Matthew A. Hodel, in an article entitled "No Hollow Hearts," written for the *American Bar Association Journal* in October 1991. Hodel is effusive in his praise for Atticus Finch as a personal and professional model: "For me, there was no more compelling model than Atticus Finch of Harper Lee's *To Kill a Mockingbird*. . . .Fine citizen, parent and lawyer, Finch skillfully defended Tom Robinson, wrongfully accused black man, and left us a story for the ages. For better or worse, Finch burdened me with the ideal that lawyering had more to do with decency than gamesmanship."[12]

The indisputable evidence of the novel's long-standing influence and its currency can be found in 1992, when, one might argue, Atticus Finch himself was accused and tried in the popular legal press. Finch, the small-town lawyer who had been accused by his townspeople in 1935 of excessive love of black people, was in 1992 being charged with racism. On this occasion, more than 30 years after the publication of *TKM*, some of the best legal minds in the country rushed to the defense of Atticus. The controversy was set in motion by Monroe Freedman, a Hofstra University law professor and author of a regular column on legal ethics in *Legal Times*. In a February 1992 article entitled "Atticus Finch, R.I.P.," Freedman challenged the wisdom of upholding Harper Lee's character as a moral lawyer and worthy model on the grounds that Finch operates as a state legislator and community leader in a segregated society, living "his own life as the passive participant in that pervasive injustice."[13]

Freedman's column was so appalling to so many in the legal profession that the *New York Times* gave it news coverage, quoting two legal scholars who accused Freedman of chronological snobbery in "subjecting a New Deal–era Alabama lawyer to contemporary standards of behavior" (Margolick, 7). Another writer, R. Mason Barge, outraged by Freedman's column, responded in the 9 March 1992 *Legal Times*: "Sitting on this lofty perch of 'legal ethics,' Mr. Freedman attacks a fictional character for not attempting to change the 'racism and sexism' of a fictional town. Of course, the principal action of this rather short novel is that of a Southern lawyer placing his career and life on the line for a wrongfully accused black man."[14] Barge builds to a crescendo, continuing his assault in the context of the random violence and drugs and hunger in New York City, where Mr. Freedman practices his own profession: "I know you don't know about this, or you would be putting your butt on the line for these people instead of criticizing Atticus Finch, who did put his butt on the line for an innocent black man. Of course, he was fictional. But then so are your 'legal ethics'"

(Barge, 23). Even the president of the American Bar Association, Talbot D'Alemberte, got into the controversy by writing a letter in defense of Atticus Finch to the editor of *Legal Times* in April 1992: "Sixty years after Judge Taylor appointed Atticus Finch to defend a poor black man in *To Kill a Mockingbird*, these two fictional heroes still inspire us. Contrary to what Professor Freedman asserts, Finch rose above racism and injustice to defend the principle that all men and women deserve their day in court represented by competent counsel, regardless of their ability to pay."[15] On 27 April, still another lawyer, Timothy J. Dunn, heatedly contradicted Freedman in the *New Jersey Law Journal*, charging that Freedman erred in his denigration of "character" and "the value to the human spirit of acts of heroic value." [16]

On 18 May, Freedman had to concede that "the report in this column of the death of Atticus Finch was premature." His concession says a great deal about the enduring life of the novel: "During the past two years, this column has dealt with 'Cases and Controversies' involving unethical lawyers, dishonest judges, criminal conflicts of interest in the White House, and widespread maladministration of justice in our criminal courts. But never has there been such a fulsome response as to the column making the rather modest suggestion that a particular fictional character is not an appropriate role model for lawyers."[17] Freedman ends in puzzlement about the legal profession's "deification" and "vociferous" defense of Atticus Finch.

This heated controversy, waged in the pages of the legal press *30 years* after the publication of Harper Lee's novel, is extraordinary confirmation of the "immortality" and mythic stature of Atticus, as Freedman recognizes, and of the enduring importance of *TKM* in the individual and national consciousness.

Finally, any discussion of the book's impact has to acknowledge the immense popularity of the film, whose script was written by Horton Foote, the long-running play written by Christopher Sergel, and the 1992 television series, in which the "mockingbird" is made to sing "I'll Fly Away," an obvious and presumably unauthorized spin-off of the novel, although curiously, not one of the four *New York Times* reviews of the series from October 1991 to October 1992 makes mention of the connection.

3

The Critical and Popular Reception of
To Kill a Mockingbird

The critical assessment of *To Kill a Mockingbird* forms one of the most astonishing chapters in American literary history. The novel steadfastly maintains its position in the contemporary canon as an American masterpiece—one of the most frequently published and read books in the last 30 years. It was reviewed in at least 30 national newspapers and magazines at the time of its publication, and has since become, as we have seen, one of those texts that "makes a difference." Yet in the 33 years since its publication, it has never been the focus of a dissertation, and it has been the subject of only six literary studies, several of them no more than a couple of pages long.

The other circumstance that makes this novel's position in critical history so extraordinary is that since 1960 a greater volume of critical readings of it has been amassed by two legal scholars in law journals than by all the literary scholars in literary journals.

Its critical history, then, is baffling. Tom Shaffer, a legal scholar who has published extensively on the novel, recognizes this paradox and ventures the brief but not particularly satisfying explanation that the individual reader's intellectual response to the novel is not as immediate or as intense as other kinds of reactions—emotional, or, as Shaffer has ventured, spiritual. However, the literary historian and critic is left to explore the anomaly of the response to the novel and *how* the novel manages to elicit a particular kind of response. Finally, the question as to why a canonical novel has been neglected by literary critics has yet to be answered and can only be raised here.

In reviewing the published criticism of the novel, I will first examine the newspaper and magazine reviews that were written within a year of its publication, and then the fairly sparse literary criticism, and, finally, the legal studies the novel has generated.

THE REVIEWS

The reviews that saw print within the first year of *TKM*'s publication should be approached with the understanding that the reviewers didn't have the time or space for the reflection and expansion enjoyed by later critics writing for literary and critical journals. Yet these earlier reviews form the bulk of writing on *TKM*. The issues that catch the attention of these reviewers include the novel's difficult point of view, Lee's character development, the dark features of the narrative, the fusion of the two parts of the book and their relative merits, and the social context or message of the novel.

Lee's intricate point of view generates considerable and contradictory comment from the reviewers. Writing for *Literary Horizons* in 1960, Granville Hicks, one of the most recognized critics of the time, did not find the treatment of the point of view to be as satisfactorily executed as the rest of the novel, which he generally praises.[1] Nor is Phoebe Adams, the reviewer for the *Atlantic Monthly* satisfied with the point of view: "It is frankly and completely impossible, being told in the first person by a six-year-old girl with the prose style of a well-educated adult. Miss Lee has, to be sure, made an attempt to confine the information in the text to what Scout would actually know, but it is no more than a casual gesture toward plausibility."[2] On the other hand, Malcolm Bradbury, writing for *Punch*, has unqualified praise for the point of view: "She chooses to tell her story through the eyes of children, a strategy that I cannot normally bear because it prevents an adequate moral judgment on the fable. But Miss Lee has taken her risks and emerged triumphant."[3] Richard Sullivan of the *Chicago Sunday Tribune* is equally favorable in his assessment of the point of view: "The unaffected young narrator uses adult language to render the matter she deals with, but the point of view is cunningly restricted to that of a perceptive, independent child, who doesn't always understand fully what's happening, but who conveys completely, by implication, the weight and burden of the story."[4]

The skill with which Lee draws characters is also debated in the reviews. Although most reviewers had extremely high praise for her character development, even some friendly reviewers found some of the characters, Tom Robinson especially, to be stock ones. An otherwise favorable review in the *New York Times Literary Supplement*, for example, claims that the novel "runs the way of its many predecessors."[5] Curiously, the assessment that certain of the characters or portions of the plot are stock is never buttressed by examples of what the novel's predecessors are, or what traditions the novel so blindly follows. In the book's only negative review of any significance, Elizabeth Lee Haselden in *Christian Century* bases her objections to the novel on her assessment of the characters as types, a situation that she thinks relieves the reader from any sense of personal guilt by setting the issue of injustice at a distinct remove.

New Statesman reviewer Keith Waterhouse, one of the most perceptive readers of the novel, notices the importance in *TKM* of the children's games, which lead them and us into danger, and the inevitable attraction of the forbidden and the different: The game, he contends, is treated "forcefully" in Lee's novel, and "pretty soon we are in the adult game, based on the same fear and fascination of the dark."[6] James B. McMillan, writing for the *Alabama Review*, also notices the Gothicism present in what to the unpracticed eye is pure realism.[7]

A number of reviewers comment on the integration of the two separate parts of the book. At least two reviewers praise the first part of the book over the second, and Harding Lemay, writing for the *New York Herald Tribune*, does not find the two parts of the novel to be well integrated.[8] However, Herbert Mitgang, reviewing for the *New*

York Times, contradicts this criticism, finding that the first section of the book fully prepares one for the second section: the first part of the book leads the reader "into the heart of the story—the opening of the eyes of Southern children to the dreary facts of Negro-white injustices."[9]

Almost all of the reviewers comment on the social setting of the novel. Hicks praises Lee for her "insight into Southern mores" and her portrait of a "Southern liberal" (Hicks, 15). Bradbury also praises the author's expressed understanding of "her social scene, the American South" (Bradbury, 612). And Waterhouse writes that she does what most Americans do very badly, that is, she paints a truthful picture of a small town.

Bradbury seems to approve of what he sees as the novel's moral mission. He likes the fact that "the good stands out from the bad at all levels" (Bradbury, 612). While Sullivan, too, recognizes the "moral import" of the novel, he also underscores the fact that *TKM* "is in no way a sociological novel. It underlines no cause. It answers no questions. It offers no solutions. It proposes no programs" (Sullivan, 1). Katherine Gauss Jackson, writing for *Harper's*, also notes that Lee presents a southern situation "to which there are no easy resolutions."[10] Robert W. Henderson, on the other hand, sees in *To Kill a Mockingbird* "a most persuasive plea for racial justice."[11]

Very few reviewers venture any surmise about influences on the novel. But Phoebe Adams does note an "Alcottish" tone[12], and several other reviewers make a connection between *TKM* and the work of Carson McCullers, particularly *Member of the Wedding*.

For the most part, then, the reviews are noteworthy only for throwing light on the reception of a first novel by a southerner at an intense moment in civil rights history. Some students will find the fact that the reviewers scarcely acknowledge the pertinent historical moment, into which the novel emerges, more interesting than what those reviewers actually do say. For this reason, the old argument that the reviewers reveal more about themselves than they do about Harper Lee's *TKM* can be made with some confidence.

Because of their brevity and superficiality, several of the critical studies of the novel are scarcely more useful to a serious reader than are the reviews. The earliest literary effort to treat Harper Lee as a subject of scholarship was actually a note in *American Notes and Queries*, a journal in which one- to three-page pieces of scholarship appear. The piece contains very little about her famous novel. Written by W. U. McDonald, Jr., the piece is a summary of Lee's satiric writing for her college's humor magazine. Two of the college pieces cited by McDonald hold interest for the study of her later novel: one is a satiric essay on the successful writer, and the other is a one-act play satirizing Alabama politics.[13] Jill P. May's study of censorship, cited in chapter 2, includes only a very brief critical analysis of the novel, and the criticism of *TKM* in W. J. Stuckey's *The Pulitzer Prize Novels: A Critical Backward Look* is also only a few paragraphs long, and its point is that Lee is an exceptionally talented writer whose novel is much more skillfully executed than many other Pulitzer Prize books; still, he concludes, the novel isn't of the quality that merits the prize. Stuckey's assessment is largely negative, following his thesis that the best fiction is usually overlooked by the Pulitzer committee. He quarrels with the book's "moral," the rendering of its point of view, and the "sentimental" statement of the problem of black people in Alabama. Nevertheless, Stuckey concedes that *TKM* has its strengths, including some "well executed" scenes, "suggesting that Harper Lee has more talent for writing fiction than a number of more famous Pulitzer winners."[14]

The next critical study is a distinct disappointment that scarcely merits the title of critical literary study. William Going's "Store and Mockingbird: Two Pulitzer Novels about the South" is primarily a summary of *TKM* and T. S. Stribling's *The Store* and a superficial comparison of the two: Going's conclusion is that both narratives include comments on family life, education, legal entanglements, small towns, and black characters.[15]

In addition to this criticism, in the 33 years since the novel's publication, only four other studies have achieved the status of literary or critical analyses of *TKM*. Two of these were authored by Fred Erisman—one in 1973 in the *Alabama Review*, and one in 1981 in the *Journal of Regional Culture*. An article by R. A. Dave appeared in *Indian Studies in American Fiction* in 1974. Portions of the latest study, an analysis by Claudia Durst Johnson in *Studies in American Fiction*, are included in the last chapter of this book.[16]

Fred Erisman's thesis in "The Romantic Regionalism of Harper Lee" is that the author posits the replacement of the "archaic, imported romanticism" of the past with a newer, Emersonian romanticism, which rests on the higher principles of the present moment. It is chiefly through the character of Atticus Finch that Emersonian idealism is made manifest: in a transcendental way, Atticus is a nonconformist and a skeptic about the past. The novel is a promise, Erisman argues, that a new, less destructive regionalism will emerge as the romanticism of Ralph Waldo Emerson replaces the romanticism of Sir Walter Scott.

Like Erisman's work, R. A. Dave's "*To Kill a Mockingbird*: Harper Lee's Tragic Vision," unusually rich with allusions, is a valuable disclosure of the intricate meanings of *mockingbird*, which Dave plays out against Walt Whitman's "Out of the Cradle Endlessly Rocking" with its "two feather'd guests from Alabama." His analysis of the connotation of the names in the novel is also enlightening: Ewell is almost a homophone for evil; the Finches are also like the mockingbirds in the novel; Jem and Scout "evoke a sense of value and selfless service." Dave also makes compelling connections between Lee's novel as autobiography and Charles Dickens's David Copperfield and James Joyce's Stephen Dedalus; between the regionalism of the novel and that in the novels of Jane Austen, Thomas Hardy, and Mark Twain; between the tone and techniques of the novel and those in Harriet Beecher Stowe's *Uncle Tom's Cabin*; between the pathos of the novel and that of a Greek tragedy.

THE LEGAL CRITICISM

Some of the more interesting criticism of the novel, and certainly the largest volume of commentary on the novel, has been done by legal rather than literary scholars. Chief among these is Thomas Shaffer, a professor of law at Notre Dame University. He consistently uses the character of Atticus Finch in his prodigious published scholarship and in his classroom, to explore "legal morality." As Shaffer writes, "The most persistently useful textbook I have used in teaching legal ethics is Harper Lee's *To Kill a Mockingbird*."[17] Shaffer's work is at the center of no small amount of legal controversy over the merits of "character," "Christianity," "morality," and "gentlemanliness" in a lawyer, Shaffer seeing Atticus Finch as an exemplar. Shaffer's basic question in his several works on morality is: "Is it possible to be a good person and a good lawyer?" Morality, he argues, comes from long-ingrained character; from what we absorb over the years from narratives of morality; from our intricate moral connections with family, church, and community—not from legal codes. Beyond this, the hero is one who, like Atticus, has greater insight and bravery than the rest of us, whose efforts are extraordinary and beyond what can be explained rationally, and whose dedication to the truth is fostered by the religious community. The problem Shaffer acknowledges is that Atticus's devotion to the truth and his genteelness get in the way of his defense of Tom Robinson. Had he been less of a gentleman, his cross-examination of Mayella Ewell may have been more effective in revealing, for example, the father-daughter incest. Had he been less devoted to the truth, Atticus might have left unsaid or unexplored truths that were guaranteed to enrage the jury against Robinson, such as the sexual nature of Mayella's advances. Although Shaffer's implication is that Atticus is a hero because he doesn't veer from his ingrained truthfulness and gentlemanliness even to avert his client's tragic fate, Shaffer is not clear about his conclusions, as one of his critics has written.[18]

Shaffer also makes the puzzling statement that Atticus is wrong in his handling of the Boo Radley incident, presumably by not having Boo arrested. Nevertheless, he argues, it is a mistake that does not diminish him as a hero. Attorney Timothy Hall of the University of Mississippi Law School allies himself with Shaffer when he argues that rather than growing out of codes and rules, ethical conduct grows out of "character," which he defines, using Atticus as the example, as "a reservoir of moral faculties and dispositions." Atticus's courage and ethics before and during the trial "would have to be pulled out of the storehouse" of his past. Hall, like Shaffer, argues that the limits that character places on behavior may result in a diminished defense of a client, but, like Shaffer, he makes no clear judgment about which role a lawyer should choose. Atticus's life teaches us, Hall argues, that even if we can't teach morality, we can make clear how virtue and character operate in the practice of law, that they are not irrelevant, and that we need not "banish feeling and emotion from the classroom."[19]

Shaffer and Hall, who make frequent references to *TKM* in their scholarship, have their detractors, especially among those lawyers who maintain the pressing need for a strong code of ethics and whose positions arise from more rational, as opposed to transcendental, arguments. John Ayer, in his review of Shaffer's work for the *Journal of Legal Education*, argues that Shaffer and Hall never commit themselves about legal quandaries; that moral narratives, like those scattered throughout *TKM*, are not absolutes, but are open to interpretation; and that Shaffer, in particular, is puzzling and off-putting in his repeated intrusive testimonies to his own Christianity. Certainly, I would argue that Shaffer's contention that Atticus's heroism arises in large measure from the religious society that surrounds him is scarcely supported by a text that portrays the church chiefly as the repository for an evil-spirited missionary society; pulpits accustomed to woman bashing; primitive Baptists who excoriate one of the few admirable characters in the novel for her love of flowers; and a couple whose narrow religion has led them to lock their son away from the light of day for his entire adult life.

In summary, then, the novel's critical history has taken unorthodox turns. In essence, the pattern of that history as a whole is more interesting than its individual parts.

READINGS

4

The Boundaries of Form

To Kill a Mockingbird is the story of the relationship between three children, Scout and Jem Finch and their friend Dill, in a small town in southern Alabama, and the effect that their eccentric neighbors and a black man's trial for rape has on them. It is essentially a tale about a variety of boundaries—those of race, region, time, class, sex, tradition, and code—boundaries that are at times threatening to collapse, that are threatened by circumstances and community members. The subject of boundaries gives form to the following reading of *TKM*. Chapter 4 is a discussion of the technical boundaries that the author has established to advance her narrative, that is, matters of plot, point of view, setting, and metaphor. Chapter 5 is a discussion of the novel's use of the Gothic tradition, a fictional construct of walls, epitomized by the dark castle. Chapter 6 becomes more particular, with an examination of the walls of difference that separate characters. The boundaries of law and code are the subjects of chapter 7, and the concluding chapter, chapter 8, explores the relationship of art and expression to the boundaries discussed earlier.

The narrative is divided into two parts: the first primarily documents the children's obsession with Arthur "Boo" Radley, a reclusive neighbor whom they have never seen, and the second chiefly describes their father's defense of Tom Robinson, a black man accused of raping a white woman. Several episodes in which the children encounter the strange, sometimes evil reality outside the slow, Edenic existence of their own house form the structure of the novel's two parts. The major episodes of part one include Scout's first encounter with school; the children's play about the Radleys; Scout's first snow; her neighbor's fire; the Christmas the children receive rifles as presents; Atticus's shooting of a mad dog; and Jem's reading sessions with the neighbor Mrs. Dubose, a morphine addict. The major episodes in part two include a black church service that the children attend with their housekeeper, Calpurnia; the introduction into their household of their Aunt Alexandra; an encounter with a lynch mob; the trial of Tom Robinson; the narrator's afternoon with her Aunt Alexandra's missionary society; and the final episode, in which the children are saved by Boo Radley from Bob Ewell's attack. The thread that runs through all the episodes is the subject of difference, whether it be the difference of race (as with Tom Robinson, the black congregation, and Calpurnia), or social deviation (as in the case of Boo Radley, Mrs. Dubose, the Ewells, and Dolphus Raymond, whom they meet at the trial), or the pronounced differences that Scout discovers between herself and other, proper young ladies.

THE PLOT AND SETTING

The novel is initially introduced through a dialogue between Jem, the older brother, and Scout, the narrator, who as adults try to sort out the childhood experiences that form the narrative of the novel, just as in their youthful years they explored between them the irrational society of which they were a part—sometimes discussing their father and the upcoming trial, sometimes discussing Aunt Alexandra's definition of family.

The story is told by the adult woman, the young protagonist Scout grown up, who is looking back on her childhood during the time of her last summer before entering grammar school, up to the late fall of her third year in school. Still, the point of view comes from the child's consciousness, and events of the past are related largely within the boundaries of what the child of six, seven, and eight knows. Little in the way of an adult tone or adult wisdom, with its cynicism, judgments, and moralizing, is allowed to pollute the observations of a very precocious child. Even the narrative voice is largely the child's, though lacking is the self-consciously naive language drawing attention to itself, as in, for example, Mark Twain's *The Adventures of Huckleberry Finn* or J.D. Salinger's *The Catcher in the Rye*. Nor can one classify the point of view as ironic in the traditional sense, as one finds irony in Twain and Salinger, or in stories like Ring Lardner's "Haircut," Eudora Welty's "Why I Live at the P.O.," and William Faulkner's version of "Spotted Horses," with its first-person narration. For, though the tone is childlike, the reader is prone to trust the judgments and values of the narrator.

Like many great novels, from Leo Tolstoy's *War and Peace* to James Joyce's *Ulysses*, the universality of *To Kill a Mockingbird* arises from its regional characters and plot, encapsulated in a distinctive time and place. The action, which begins in 1933 and takes place primarily in 1935, occurs during the nation's great depression and recovery. There are references to the national situation; to Franklin Roosevelt's declaration that we have nothing to fear but fear itself; to the economic crash that hit the cotton-dependent areas of the South especially hard; to the Works Progress Administration (the WPA), designed by the Roosevelt administration to put people back to work in federally financed jobs; to the NRA, the National Recovery Act, Roosevelt's plan for economic recovery from the depression, and to its dismantling by a ruling of "the nine old men" of the Supreme Court of the United States. There are references to sit-down strikes and breadlines in the cities, and growing poverty in the country; to payments for professional services in goods rather than cash (Atticus tells the children that the doctor delivers babies for sacks of potatoes); to the growing menace of fascism in Germany, ("how can Hitler just put a lot of folks in a pen like that" [*TKM*, 245]); and to Mrs. Eleanor Roosevelt ("I think that woman, that Mrs. Roosevelt's lost her mind—just plain lost her mind coming down to Birmingham and tryin' to sit with 'em" [*TKM*, 234]). There is a further topical reference, also to a changing South, in Atticus's recommendation to Jem of the speeches of Henry Grady, editor of the *Atlanta Journal*, a progressive thinker for his time, who advocated greater justice in the South's dealings with its black citizens (*TKM*, 146).

But, as the narrator notes, "these were events remote from the world" of the novel's children (*TKM*, 12). Maycomb is geographically and politically isolated, and placed too far away from the river and the north end of the county to expand: "The town remained the same size for a hundred years, an island in a patch work sea of cotton fields and timberland" (*TKM*, 131). Indeed, the adults, the children, and the town itself seem suspended in time, somehow outside the wrenching economic and political agony of the larger world of the nation in the 1930s: "There was no hurry, for there was nowhere to go, nothing to buy and no money to buy it with, nothing to see outside the boundaries of Maycomb County" (*TKM*, 5). Their small town in the midst of a rural economy seems as close to the 1880s as to the 1930s, just as the community of Finch's Landing, the ancestral seat established by the family's slave-holding ancestor, is closer to the town of Maycomb, where they live, than to Birmingham or Mobile or Montgomery, where their father serves as a legislator. An image of this tired old town, as the narrator calls it, could have served well to illustrate a nineteenth-century scene: "Mules hitched to Hoover carts flicked flies in the sweltering shade of the live oaks in the square" (*TKM*, 5). Still, the hard times experienced by the rural whites seem to exacerbate racial tension in the form of an escalation of competition for work alluded to in the resentment Tom Robinson's widow encounters in looking for a job.

The location or place is as central to the meaning of the novel as are its plot and characters. The small southern Alabama town is set apart, not only from other regions in the nation, but from other parts of Alabama. Unlike Montgomery and Mobile, Maycomb and its environs have been bypassed by growth, despite its founders' anticipation that it would grow into one of the state's business centers. Also, unlike the northern part of the state, with its liquor interests, Republicans, and professors, Maycomb's is a land-based economy. Even its physical appearance is defined by its warm climate. For example, the inhabitants, having no need of cellars, build their houses above the ground.

Details of setting take on symbolic weight. Maycomb is a place where large old trees prevent the growth of grass, and many yards are frequently swept dirt: "Maycomb was an old town, but it was a tired old town when I first knew it. In rainy weather the streets turned to red slop; grass grew on the sidewalks, the courthouse sagged in the square. Somehow, it was hotter then: a black dog suffered on a summer's day; bony mules hitched to Hoover carts flicked flies in the sweltering shade of the live oaks on the square" (*TKM*, 5). The ancient trees, especially around the house of the eccentric Radley family, are like the persistent past itself, and block the sun and all the present-day realities it represents from entering the places underneath, thereby allowing very little to flourish or change—certainly not the attitudes in this place that has been shaped irrevocably by a plantation system, the Civil War, and a cotton-based economy.

Its southernness is fantastic, and is characterized by its exotic camellias; its long, hot summers, in which the action of most of the chapters take place; and its lack of snow. Azaleas flourish near the houses. The madness of summer even intrudes on February in the form of a mad dog. It takes someone like Atticus, something of an anomaly in his community, to take on the mad dog, just as he will confront the racial madness of Maycomb, Old Sarum, and Bob Ewell, its most notorious inhabitant.

IMAGES AND SYMBOLS

The chief symbol of the novel, cited in the title, is the mockingbird, first mentioned in their father's instructions to Jem and Scout about the use of the air rifles he has given them for Christmas: "'I'd rather you shot at tin cans in the back yard, but I know you'll go after birds. Shoot all the blue jays you want, if you can hit 'em, but remember it's a sin to kill a mockingbird'" (*TKM*, 90). It is the first time Scout ever recalls her father naming a "sin," so she goes to their friend and neighbor, Miss Maudie, for clarification: "'Mockingbirds don't do one thing but music for us to enjoy. . . .That's why it's a sin to kill a mockingbird'" (*TKM*, 90). Another reference to the mockingbird is made in Mr. B. B. Underwood's editorial in the *Maycomb Tribune* following the shooting of Tom Robinson. As Scout explains: "Mr. Underwood simply figured it was a sin to kill cripples, be they standing, sitting, or escaping. He likened Tom's death to the senseless slaughter of songbirds by hunters and children. . . ." (*TKM*, 241). The final references to mockingbirds are specific to Boo Radley, the housebound mysterious neighbor. In the autumn after the traumatic summer of the trial and death of Tom Robinson, as the children walk past the Radley house to a night Halloween party at school, the narrator recalls, "High above us in the darkness, a solitary mocker poured out his repertoire in blissful unawareness of whose tree he sat in, plunging from the shrill kee, kee of the sunflower bird to the irascible qua-ack of a bluejay, to the sad lament of Poor Will, Poor, Poor Will" (*TKM*, 254–55). Later that night, after the children have been saved by Boo Radley from a vicious attack by Bob Ewell, Mr. Tate, the sheriff, says that identifying Boo as the murderer of Bob Ewell would be "a sin," and Scout tells Atticus, "Well, it'd be sort of like shootin' a mockingbird, wouldn't it?" (*TKM*, 276). Through these quotations the narrator invites the reader to consider the links between the harmless, vulnerable songbird and the black man, Tom Robinson, as well as the recluse Boo Radley. Like the mockingbird, both are at the mercy of the community.

The gun also takes on some symbolic value in the novel as a source of power that must always be reined in. The Ewells, recognizing no rules and feeling no charity, use their firearms to hunt out of season. Atticus, as a dead shot, has the capacity to kill mockingbirds and other harmless creatures, but refuses to hunt at all anymore, and takes up a rifle reluctantly, and only at the insistence of the sheriff, to protect the community against a mad dog. He knows that the children should have the power of the gun, but he separates himself from that power by having his brother, Jack, purchase the gun and instruct the children in its use. His chief role is to inspire them to limit their power. This is not what occurs in the case of Tom Robinson, a defenseless man with a useless arm, who is gunned down in a prison yard. A high level of civilization, of morality, is reached by the person who has the capacity to kill but chooses to place limitations on that power. When Scout asks Miss Maudie why Atticus doesn't hunt anymore, she is told, "If your father's anything, he's civilized in his heart. . . .I think maybe he put his gun down when he realized that God had given him an unfair advantage over most living things" (*TKM*, 98). Atticus refuses to take up a gun even to defend himself against Bob Ewell. And the killing of a mockingbird, that is, the Tom Robinsons and Boo Radleys of the world, goes beyond legalities to morality. It is not so much a crime as it is a sin.

The figure of the mockingbird is reinforced by the realization that from the novel's inception Boo Radley and Tom Robinson are caged birds. Throughout most of the novel, Tom is in a literal prison— first in the Maycomb County jail and then in the state penitentiary, where he is shot when he attempts to fly. Boo is imprisoned in his house by his father.

When the mockingbird of the title is mentioned in the novel, it is associated with song. The characters who are literally singing birds are the members of Calpurnia's congregation, who amaze Scout and Jem when "miraculously on pitch, a hundred voices sang out" and "music swelled around us" (*TKM*, 121). The two most obvious mockingbirds, Tom Robinson and Boo Radley, are not literally singers, but they convey song stories through the lives that they live: Tom the black man and Boo the recluse singing through their lives of mystery and gentleness. The urge to sing and fly freely is not restricted to these imprisoned mockingbirds, for in many ways all the novel's characters are mockingbirds, trapped by place and the past, their songs being the stories they live, their attempts at flight being small rebellions against different kinds of convention.

The narrator, herself, is the singing mockingbird, joined in story with Tom Robinson and Boo Radley and others, conveying their different songs as she sings first the song of one bird, then that of another. The novel itself is the mockingbird song—ironically (though the novelist would not have known it, though she might have predicted it) silenced on occasion by attempts to censor it.

Just as the title brings the reader toward the novel's meaning, so does the epigraph from Charles Lamb: "Lawyers, I suppose, were children once"; for much of the novel has to do with the interplay of childhood and adulthood. Though childhood seems at times idealized, as when the children play imaginatively in carefree summertime, it is also cruel, insensitive, and the epitome of ignorance: the children make the tragedy of the Radleys the public subject of their dramas; Scout gives the Cunningham child a pounding for inadvertently causing her trouble on the first day of school, and later embarrasses him at her own dinner table; the children make fun of Mr. Avery through a snowman parody, constructed in the front yard for the amusement of the street; Scout contemplates "mashing" a roly-poly bug. What keeps these two children from practicing the same cruelty as the other children is a father, a supreme adult, who speaks to them as adults.

Yet it is not natural childhood that is destructive so much as it is the community decision to deny adulthood to its mature citizens. Every member of the black race is denied intellectual adulthood by the white community. Boo Radley is denied adulthood by his family. For in adulthood there is power. This alone explains why some of the novel's mature men and women are kept in continual childhood. Note, for example, how "Mr.," an address of respect accorded adult males, is even bestowed on the adolescent Jem, but denied the grown man, Tom. The two Finch children and Dill, in sharing a certain vulnerability, feel kinship to those like Tom Robinson and Boo Radley, from whom the power of adulthood is withheld by the community.

These, then, are the confines of the narrative: the boundaries of the action, the limits of the voice, the restrictions of time and place, and the chief defining symbols with which the novel is introduced—the mockingbird and the child.

5

The Gothic Tradition

The twentieth-century American South is as much a repository of the Gothic tradition in literature as is eighteenth- and nineteenth-century England. Both the forms and themes of *To Kill a Mockingbird* partake of the Gothic tradition at the same time that the novel engages the Gothic as a subject for critical commentary, or, one might even say, for satire, in the manner of Jane Austen's *Northanger Abbey*. The word Gothic is itself used to describe both Dill's worst performance in the Radley dramas and the courthouse architecture. An examination of the incorporation into the novel of the more superficial trappings of the Gothic, as well as the centrality to the novel of modern Gothic's social and psychological significance, opens up the text for serious readers, guiding them toward two critical considerations in the text, which will form the two major divisions in this study: the confrontation of the unknown Alien or Other in the process of self-definition, and the power and significance of legal boundaries in the life and mind of the community.

The Character of the Gothic

The penchant for classifying such a large body of recent southern fiction as Gothic, including the works of Truman Capote, much of whose work is seen as solidly in the new Gothic tradition and whose name is linked to Harper Lee's, should caution the reader of *TKM* against making hasty and unwarranted assumptions about Lee's novel automatically belonging in the Gothic tradition. However, an examination of the external characteristics of both the traditional and modern Gothic novel is sufficient to support such a classification. To determine just what the characteristics of the Gothic are, it is instructive to turn to recent scholarship on the subject by David Punter, Kate Ferguson Ellis, Eugenia C. DeLamotte, Eve Sedgwick, Maurice Levy, William Patrick Day, Terry Heller, and Irving Malin. These scholars understand Gothic subjects to include murders, ghosts, witches, werewolves, vampires, monsters, imprisonment, ruins, nostalgia for the past, unnatural parents, haunted or decayed quarters, specters, forebodings, deformity, madness, magic, dark and forbidding secrets, sexual violence, rape, incest, insanity, mental breakdown, and cultural decay. David Punter summarizes the characteristics of Gothic fiction as "an emphasis on portraying the terrifying, a common insistence on archaic setting, a prominent use of the supernatural, the presence of highly stereotyped characters and the attempt to develop and perfect techniques of literary suspense. . . .The repetition of 'horror' and 'horrible'; the 'total darkness' and the 'masked faces' of the villains; the black-and-white tone of 'unmerited persecution'; the insistence on the potential finality of the imprisonment; the note of half-gasping, half-gloating voyeurism—all are commonplaces of the genre."[1]

To this definition, Kate Ferguson Ellis and Maurice Levy add and emphasize the importance of the failed home, and Levy specifically adds the importance of architecture as a repository of the pernicious past and of institutional power.[2] Eugenia C. DeLamotte stresses that the Gothic vision has always focused on social relations and social institutions.[3] And William Patrick Day underscores the Gothic characteristics of the anticonventional vision of reality; fantasies; transformation; metamorphosis; doubling; and oppositions of good and evil, love and hate, pain and pleasure, the objective and the subjective, cause and effect, masculine and feminine. To this he adds the argument that the Gothic is opposed to the Romantic view of the sublime.[4]

Virtually every external feature of the Gothic can be located in *To Kill a Mockingbird*, either as part of the action of the novel, or as an operative element in the children's imaginations. There are the forebodings of evil in the unseasonable snow, the mad dog in the street, and various ominous secrets. Miss Maudie says, "The things that happen to people we never really know. What happens in houses behind closed doors, what secrets—" (*TKM*, 50). Dill's imaginative creations are pure Gothic, as is graphically illustrated by his explanation of why he has run away from home. Scout relays the story: "Having been bound in chains and left to die in the basement. . .by his new father, who disliked him, and secretly kept alive on raw field peas by a passing farmer who heard his cries for help (the good man poked a bushel pod by pod through the ventilator), Dill worked himself free by pulling the chains from the wall. Still in wrist manacles, he wandered two miles out of Meridian where he discovered a small animal show and was immediately engaged to wash the camel" (*TKM*, 140). The most persistent Gothic element in the novel is the presence of witches, ghosts, vampires, and other forms of the supernatural, all of which excite the fear and terror that accompany the Gothic scene. The children, and even some of the town's adults, view Boo Radley as a ghost or vampire or witch to whom they attribute bloodlettings and blood sucking, as well as a host of minor incidents, unnatural and foul. Further mystery surrounds him as stories tell of his wanderings at night, during which he peeps into the windows of southern ladies. This monster, whose face reportedly looks like a skull, is a horror to behold: "Boo was about six-and-a-half feet tall, judging from his tracks; he dined on raw squirrels and any cats he could catch, that's why his hands were blood-stained—if you ate an animal raw, you could never wash his blood off. There was a long jagged scar that ran across his face; what teeth he had were yellow and rotten; his eyes popped, and he drooled most of the time" (*TKM*, 13). Not only has his awful punishment "turned him into a ghost" as Atticus says, the knowledge of his punishment has transformed him in the eyes of the town into "a malevolent phantom" (*TKM*, 43).

Boo's activities are very like those generally attributed to a community of witches:

> People said he went out at night when the moon was down, and peeped in windows. When people's azaleas froze in a cold snap, it was because he breathed on them. Any stealthy small crimes committed in Maycomb were his work. Once the town was terrorized by a series of morbid nocturnal events: people's chickens and household pets were found mutilated; although the culprit was Crazy Addie, who eventually drowned himself in Barker's Eddy, people still looked at the Radley Place, unwilling to discard their initial suspicions. A Negro would not pass the Radley Place at night, he would cut across to the sidewalk opposite and whistle as he walked. The Maycomb school grounds adjoined the back of the Radley lot; from the Radley chicken yard tall pecan trees shook their fruit into the school yard, but the nuts lay untouched by the children: Radley pecans would kill you. A baseball hit into the Radley yard was a lost ball and no questions asked. (*TKM*, 9)

The Gothic supernatural, belief in which the children frequently attribute to black people alone, lingers at the back of the children's minds. Although they have been educated to disdain the belief in "hotsteams," those ghosts upon which the unsuspecting person can stumble on a lonely road, the children often speak of them with horror and dread.

The Architecture of the Gothic

Very prominent in the novel is the Gothic presence of the decayed and haunted structure, in this case, both the Radley and Dubose houses. Maurice Levy finds that architecture is the key to the Gothic, embodying shadow, antiquity, mystery and ruin, and acting as repositories of the past and of institutions. Jem, pointing out the Radley house, explains to Walter Cunningham, "A hain't lives there" (*TKM*, 23).

Walter already knows about the "pizened" pecans from the Radley's tree. Jem will remind Scout of the Radley poison when she chews the gum she found in the tree: "Don't you know you're not supposed to even touch the trees over there? You'll get killed if you do!" (*TKM*, 33). Both the Dubose and Radley houses fit the pattern of the architecture of fear, harboring what appear to be forbidden secrets and embodying the degeneracy of the past. The Radley house and grounds, in particular, are, in the minds of the children, haunted places of palpable evil and danger. The front of the Radley house is a forbidding ghost house: "The house was low, was once white with a deep front porch and green shutters, but had long ago darkened to the color of the slate-gray yard around it. Rain-rotted shingles drooped over the eaves of the veranda; oak trees kept the sun away. The remains of a picket drunkenly guarded the front yard—a "swept" yard that was never swept—where johnson grass and rabbit-tobacco grew in abundance" (*TKM*, 8). The back of the Radley House is as imposingly fearful as the front: "A ramshackle porch ran the width of the house; there were two doors and two dark windows between the doors. Instead of a column, a rough two-by-four supported one end of the roof. An old Franklin stove sat in a corner of the porch; above it a hat-rack mirror caught the moon and shone eerily" (*TKM*, 52). The Dubose house, equally ominous, is linked to the haunted Radley house. When Jem complains that the Dubose house is "all creepy" and that "there's shadows and things on the ceiling," Atticus replies, "That should appeal to your imagination. Just pretend you're inside the Radley house" (*TKM*, 105). Scout will record her firsthand view of the Dubose house: "An oppressive odor met us when we crossed the threshold, an odor I had met many times in rain-rotted gray houses where there are coal-oil lamps, water dippers, and unbleached domestic sheets. It always made me afraid, expectant, watchful" (*TKM*, 106).

Nowhere in the novel does architecture carry a more heavy symbolic burden as a repository of a past that won't die than in the description of the Maycomb County courthouse. Its ancient outsized pillars are symbols of the antebellum South, dinosaurs that have survived and been retained even after the rest of the courthouse burned down before the Civil War. Referring to columns or pillars as symbols of the plantation South, Virginia Hamilton writes in *Alabama: A Bicentennial History*, that "columns are essential to the aura of a southern mansion; remove them and only a large box remains. . . . If fronted only by a row of white wooden columns, the plainest country house gives off an air of importance and authority" (Hamilton, 108). It is not insignificant that the trustees of Alabama's major university, the University of Alabama (which Harper Lee attended), are rumored to have required columns on any campus building they were expected to approve for construction, a story given credibility by the columns attached to a round biological sciences building constructed in the 1970s. The newer courthouse in fictional Maycomb, like the post–Civil War South, is smaller than the original edifice, but is, nevertheless, built around the pillars. As *TKM*'s narrator clarifies, "It is better to say, built in spite of them" (*TKM*, 162).

The building is a monstrosity, a haphazard combination of architectural elements: a Victorian tower violently affixed to the old Greek revival columns. The courthouse structure's link to the past is secured with the comment that the clock in the courthouse is rusty and does not work, a characteristic somehow appropriate in a community where time seems so often to stand still. As the narrator relates, the courthouse's present state is symbolic of the people it serves, "a people determined to preserve every physical scrap of the past" (*TKM*, 162).

This architectural monument to and repository of the South houses age and decay: "sunless county cubbyholes," "dim hutches," "decaying record books," "damp cement," and "stale urine." The "grey-faced men" who work there are barely human, barely alive (Scout calls them "creatures"). Like their dark workplace, they too seem imprisoned in the nineteenth century, almost as impervious to change and seasons, as removed from light and life, as Count Dracula himself (*TKM*, 162–63).

The courthouse's hodgepodge architecture is also emblematic of the system of justice it houses, where vestiges of antebellum legal inequality remain as surely as the Greek revival pillars.

The Maycomb jail is another Gothic architectural statement that even the narrator describes as "a miniature Gothic joke." In every way the pretense at grandeur and Gothic terror in the building is undercut by the ridicule it invites. It is "the most vulnerable and hideous of the county's buildings." It is both hideously venerable and a joke, for it looks like a "Victorian privy" (*TKM*, 150). Though it has tiny battlements and flying buttresses in the Gothic vein, it is only one cell wide and two cells high. While its pretentious Gothicism would call for a lonely setting on a hill, it is instead sandwiched between a hardware store and the newspaper office. And its lopsided design bespeaks a lopsided corrections system, in that only black prisoners are incarcerated there, as if only black people committed crimes in Maycomb County. After Boo Radley stabs his father in the leg, he is imprisoned in the courthouse basement in order to segregate him from the black prisoners. The foul, damp basement air is judged to be less injurious to the young white man than having to share a cell with a black man. Fittingly, those who approve of the jail's bizarre design also approve of the skewed justice carried out inside its cells.

First Purchase African M.E. Church, like Maycomb's other buildings—its courthouse and jail—embodies essential, inexplicable conflicts, largely arising from and reflecting a system of inequality and segregation. On Sunday it is a place of worship for the black community, and on weekdays it is a gambling den for white men.

GOTHIC BREAKDOWN

Other Gothic themes in *TKM* are insanity, mental breakdown, and degeneration. As usual, there is an inversion in the novel: the so-called sane are insane and the reputedly insane are saner than the rest. The subjects of sanity and insanity are woven throughout the novel, working with the themes of the Other, of civilization, and courage. These themes are most prominent, of course, in Boo Radley, who, having been incarcerated for most of his life, in a moment of madness stabs his father in the leg with scissors for no immediately discernable reason. Scout discusses Boo's sanity with Miss Maudie. To keep him from being sent to Tuscaloosa, the site of the state mental hospital, he is further confined for the rest of his life in a smaller domestic asylum, over which his father and then his brother preside as wardens. After the children's attempt to peek at him through the window, Scout believes that Boo is insane and after them: "Insects splashing against the screen were Boo Radley's insane fingers picking the wire to pieces" (*TKM*, 55). And Jem later says, "'He's crazy, I reckon, like they say'" (*TKM*, 72).

The Finches themselves have had a distant cousin locked up in the state mental institution. Cousin Joshua, who according to Aunt Alexandra, was "a beautiful character," was locked up after attempting to shoot the university's president. And the narrative presents us with others who at the very least operate on the borders of sanity, notably, Mrs. Henry Lafayette Dubose, and "Crazy Addie," whose insane antics are blamed on Boo.

Yet these cases pale in comparison with the other cases of insanity: the marginal insanity of people loose in the community, like Bob Ewell, and the occasional insanity that overtakes the whole community at times, especially apparent in the behavior of the inhabitants of Old Sarum and in the meeting of the missionary society. Indeed, the Tom Robinson trial is an insane episode in the lives of the community, an episode foreshadowed by the mad dog entering the quiet street. Atticus says to his brother Jack during the Christmas before the trial, "Why reasonable people go stark raving mad when anything involving a Negro comes up, is something I don't pretend to understand" (*TKM*, 88).

The Gothic Past

One of the strongest Gothic subjects in *TKM* is the undue force that a baneful past exercises on the present. David Punter writes of the Gothic that "ghost stories, surely, have *always* been vehicles for nostalgia, attempts to understand the past, and the glance over the shoulder is their central motif and embodiment" (Punter, 425). The past of the region, and certain attitudes towards the past, have shaped Maycomb County and impinge on its characters and the novel's action. The Finches, Scout explains, were always southerners, and "being Southerners, it was a source of shame to some members of the family that we had no recorded ancestors on either side of the Battle of Hastings" (*TKM*, 3). The power that the South's distant past exercises on life in the 1930s is demonstrated by the narrator, who, taking a "broad view" of causes and effects, claims that the events recounted in the novel were a direct result of the plantation past: "It really began with Andrew Jackson" (*TKM*, 3). Like the Finches, most of the white townspeople are descendants of slave-holding English immigrants, and most have been rendered poor by the Civil War. A relative and veteran of the Civil War, Cousin Ike Finch, who lives in Maycomb County, speaks of the Missouri Compromise and the deeds of Stonewall Jackson as if they were current events, reminding Atticus's family of the early Civil War, and foreshadowing a local civil war over a black man being charged with rape. Aunt Alexandra is a typical proponent of the need to keep the past alive, to imbue the children with the family's history. It is she who insists that family quality is determined by the past, by how old a family is.

It is the past of racial divisions and the genteel life that lingers most glaringly in the attitudes of the area's citizens, as Atticus confesses to Scout in the winter before the trial, when he says that he will probably lose the case "simply because we were licked a hundred years before we started," referring to the plantation mentality (*TKM*, 76). White attitudes toward blacks in Maycomb, having been shaped by slavery and reconstruction, have changed very little over the years. And it is not just the illiterate rural poor who are cursed with a past of racism. The upstanding community of the town is also heir to the same past. The missionary society ladies continue fighting the Civil War in terms of race at their meeting, calling the "Yankees" hypocrites: "People up there set 'em free, but you don't see 'em settin' at the table with 'em (*TKM*, 234). These genteel ladies consider the accused black man's wife to be beyond salvation, and their leader, Scout's Aunt Alexandra, refuses to allow Scout to visit the home of the black woman who has reared them.

Nor, with the exception of the three children who are markedly untypical, does the younger generation show promise of being liberated from its racist past, in part because that past is bestowed upon them by their teachers and parents. Francis, Scout's and Jem's unsavory cousin, echoes his own grandparent's biases in taunting his cousins about their father: "'Grandma says it's bad enough he lets you run wild, but now he's turned out a nigger-lover we'll never be able to walk the streets of Maycomb agin. He's ruinin' the family, that's what he's doin'" (*TKM*, 83). Similarly, a child living in town, Cecil Jacobs, has had his parents' attitudes passed along to him: "'My folks said your daddy was a disgrace an' that nigger oughta hang from the water-tank'" (*TKM*, 76). Later, in the classroom, Cecil will be utterly confused by Hitler's persecution of the Jews: "'They're white, ain't they?'" (*TKM*, 245). The assumptions are not questioned by his teacher, Miss Gates, whose own opinions Scout has heard outside the courtroom: "I heard her say it's time somebody taught 'em a lesson, they were gettin' way above themselves, an' the next thing they think they can do is marry us" (*TKM*, 247).

Mrs. Lafayette Dubose, a repugnant old woman who reputedly sleeps with a Confederate States of America pistol, and to whom Jem must read *Ivanhoe*, is in many ways the epitome of the worn-out, old southern past. She is sick, dying, bitter, racist, out of touch with reality, and wrapped up in her morphine-clouded, tattered romantic world. It is no accident that *Ivanhoe*, reputedly the shaper of the plantation attitude, is the novel she wants to hear Jem read. This aristocratic old woman, whose very name denotes "Old Family," is just as vitriolic about race as are those called white trash: "'Yes, indeed, what has this world come to when a Finch goes against his raising?. . .Your father's no better than the niggers and trash he works for!'" (*TKM*, 102). Ironically, Mrs. Dubose is dependent on a black woman, Jessie, to keep her alive by nursing her, administering her morphine when she wants it, and helping her through the excruciating process of withdrawal. Mrs. Dubose's camellias, especially her Snow-on-the-Mountain, are as much symbols of the old South as she is, an assumption corroborated by the fact that Jem cuts them down in retaliation for the old woman's persistence in calling Atticus an enemy of the old South. Alabama historian Virginia Hamilton writes that a particularly violent group of southern vigilantes, given to lynching and terrorizing the black populace after the Civil War as a way of preserving the old southern way of life, called themselves the Knights of the White Camellia (Hamilton, 86). Mrs. Dubose dies, but the camellias persist. She tells Jem just before she dies, "'Thought you could kill my Snow-on-the-Mountain, didn't you? Well, Jessie says the top's growing back out,'" and right on top of that remark she adds, "'Don't guess you feel like holding it [his head] up, though, with what your father is'" (*TKM*, 110). It is probably no accident that the most racist character in the novel is given a name associated with old South gentility—Robert E. Lee Ewell. In typical Gothic fashion, *TKM* shows the ruin of a South aware of its own defeat.

Boo Radley is locked in a past that has somehow overcome entirely the flow of time. Fittingly, he gives Scout and Jem a pocket watch that will not run.

In sum, the destructive and powerful influence of the past is linked with another characteristic of the Gothic—the theme of decay and degeneration so peculiar to southern fiction. It can be seen in the physical decay of the town and its buildings, in the decline of the aristocracy (Mrs. Dubose especially, is colored, as David Punter describes the Gothic, "with the heightened hues of putrescence" [Punter, 5]), and in the degeneracy of the once well-respected Dolphus Raymond family, which, in Faulknerian fashion, has traded its gentility for racial mixing.

THE GOTHIC PRISON

The Gothic scene of imprisonment reverberates throughout the novel in literal and metaphoric ways. Central to the novel is the imprisonment of Arthur Radley in his father's house, the chief gloomy, threatening witch-house structure that was a prison even before Boo was literally locked up in it. Boo has also been imprisoned twice in the county jail, once in its basement, the modern version of a dungeon, and has lived briefly under the threat of imprisonment in Tuscaloosa's mental institution. In a very real sense, Arthur Radley, like his wild young friends, found the town of Maycomb itself and his family's narrow religion to be a prison. The children are concerned with freeing him from his house. Mayella Ewell is also a prisoner in her father's house, and Tom Robinson is imprisoned in various jails, including the one once occupied by Arthur Radley, and in a state penitentiary. The county jail, a central structure in the novel, is filled with black prisoners, and from the town's inception Tom Robinson and all of Maycomb's black citizens are imprisoned in a cage of race, as surely as Mrs. Dubose is in a prison of morphine.

Gothic imprisonment is also linked with another characteristic of the form: stereotyping. In *TKM*, the stereotype is not just a character type, but a major subject of discussion in the fiction, a commentary on a given character or group of characters who persist in stereotyping others. In this sense, the Gothic mode, with its tradition of stereotypes, becomes a subject of critical inquiry. The sophistication and humaneness, the largeness of heart and mind of any given character is shown by the degree to which he or she has moved out of a Gothic world of types to regard others as individuals and multidimensional human beings.

The reader sees characters through the eyes of young Scout, who, along with Jem and Dill, inhabit a Gothic world composed at first of a number of predictable character types. Most prominent among these is their neighbor, Arthur Radley, whom they seem to type from their readings of horror literature. Their stereotyping of Radley is illustrated in their renaming him Boo. By the novel's end, however, Boo has shed his horror story stereotype and has become a fully developed, if somewhat odd human being, who also discards the name Boo along with his one-dimensional image. Scout now addresses him respectfully as Mr. Arthur. The final effect is one of moving Arthur Radley outside of the Gothic in the mind of Scout.

Because the community never gets beyond stereotyping black people as immoral and lazy, they conveniently fail to accord them status as full human beings and adults. The residents of the poor community of Old Sarum are also generally stereotyped by the town as dirty and stupid, a view that is confounded by Mayella's love and care of geraniums: "One corner of the yard, though, bewildered Maycomb. Against the fence, in a line, were six chipped-enamel slop jars holding brilliant red geraniums, cared for as tenderly as if they belonged to

Miss Maudie Atkinson, had Miss Maudie deigned to permit a geranium on her premises. People said they were Mayella Ewell's" (*TKM*, 171). In short, the stereotypes so common to the Gothic are among those barriers that divide Maycomb society.

GOTHICISM AND THE FAMILY

Irving Malin emphasizes the theme of family, or what he calls "family terror," as a characteristic of the American Gothic. A "disfiguring love is often learned at home," he writes.[5] Kate Ferguson Ellis also sees the failed home in the Gothic as the site of terror, a place of danger and imprisonment, where some are locked in and some are locked out. Both the Radley and the Ewell families in the novel are examples of the "disfiguring love" that is "often learned at home," the Radleys sacrificing Arthur through their disfiguring love on the altar of religious fanaticism, and Mayella disfigured by the twisted love of incest. Indeed, "family" becomes a significant subject in the novel, and, as critics Ellis, Malin, and Punter point out in characterizing the Gothic, a devastatingly negative comment on the traditional family. Although *TKM* is a social novel, the story of a small-town community in the age of the traditional family, its presentation of society in the 1930s does not include a single, conventional, ideal all-American family. The biological mother has been written out of the Atticus Finch household, and is also missing from the house of Bob Ewell. The mother in the Finch family is admirably but unconventionally replaced by Calpurnia, a black woman. While Scout's and Jem's biological mother is missing from their family, Dill's biological father is missing from his. For all intents and purposes, Dill has no family at all. The whereabouts of his father is shrouded in mystery: When asked why he hasn't ever mentioned his father, Dill replies, "I haven't got one," and his further denial that his father isn't dead confounds Scout. In Dill's apparent need, he creates his own father, or at least the father he wishes he had—one who is romantic, important, and indulgent—and he tells his friends that his "father was taller than ours, he had a black beard (pointed), and was president of the L & N Railroad" (*TKM*, 36). Her despised cousin Francis tells Scout that Dill doesn't have a home: "'He just gets passed around from relative to relative'" (*TKM*, 82). Nor does Dill's mother's marriage to a man who will be his new father bring together a family for him, as Dill explains when he runs away. His mother and her new husband don't want him around: "'They stayed gone all the time, and when they were home, even, they'd get off in a room by themselves'" (*TKM*, 142–43).

There are no traditional families on the street on which the children live, not even any married couples. Scout notices that "the folks on our street are all old" (*TKM*, 90). The other neighbors are widows, unmarried women, and Mr. Avery, an unmarried man. Even Uncle Jack Finch remains unmarried. Aunt Alexandra has a husband and a married son who leaves his own son with the boy's grandparents every Christmas. Aunt Alexandra's is scarcely a conventional family unit in that she takes off, leaves her husband, and moves in with the Maycomb Finches, staying well beyond Tom Robinson's trial, which she has supposedly come to see them through. Aunt Alexandra, so strong in her obsession of remaking Atticus's unconventional family into an orthodox one and forcing the family history on the reluctant children, ironically promotes the emergence of the worst values from Atticus's family, and simultaneously threatens the existence of the best values of that family. Even though this is a family that runs to women, there is no mention by name of any female progenitor. There are only two "complete" families with two parents and children: one is that of Tom Robinson, which, because it is black, does not fit the all-American, Andy Hardy mold. The other is the Radleys' family, a weird group of religious fanatics who withdraw from the community.

Within this narrative of a community so devoid of orthodox families, the missionary society's ironic concern is for the poor Mrundas, an African tribe in which a missionary has taken an interest, who have no "sense of family." In the same ironic vein, the Atticus Finch family, which Aunt Alexandra finds so intolerably unorthodox that she must leave her own family and move in to straighten them out, is a strong and happy one, one which welcomes as one of its members a black woman, Calpurnia, as "a faithful member of this family" (*TKM*, 137).

Finally, the chief Gothic taboo is incest, which traditionally occurs between brother and sister in nineteenth-century American Gothic fiction, as found in the works of Poe, Hawthorne, and Melville. Incest is apparent in *TKM* in the intermarriage of the older generation of Finches, which Atticus calls "incest" to anger his sister, and in the father-daughter incest of the Ewells. Add to this the taboo of miscegenation, which is also central to the trial, and the Gothic subject of sexual violence present in Mayella Ewell's actual rape by her father, her sexual attraction to Tom Robinson, and her false accusation of rape by Tom.

SEXUAL ROLES

David Punter cites as one other external characteristic of Gothic fiction the "questioning of the absolute nature of sexual roles" (Punter, 411), and William Patrick Day states that, "the thematic focus of the Gothic concerns the nature of masculine and feminine identity and the nature of the family that shapes that identity" (Day, 3). This Gothic characteristic can be seen in the novel's discussions of what it means to be a "girl" and a "lady." Scout repeatedly finds oppressive, exclusionary, and puzzling the general view of what a girl and a lady should be. The "pink cotton penitentiary" begins to close in on her when her teacher and her Aunt Alexandra insist on using her gender-specific, girlish given name, Jean Louise, instead of the more neutral name that she has acquired and to which she is accustomed—Scout. Her play is the more physical, out-of-doors activity generally attributed to boys, such as tire rolling and tree climbing, and even fighting with her fists. Her language, which her Uncle Jack fails to tolerate as easily as does Atticus, is not particularly "ladylike." Her uncle chides her for her cursing, asking, "'You want to grow up to be a lady, don't you?'" When she replies in the negative, he answers, "'Of course you do'" (*TKM*, 79). She has no little girls as playmates, and seems to be truly anxious that she may be forced to find some in order to fit the gender role assigned her by the community. And instead of receiving a little girl's doll for Christmas, she gets a little boy's rifle.

Her attire of overalls is, like her name, appropriate to her activities. But, in the vein of Amelia Bloomer, her attire takes on gender-specific political overtones. Her overalls are the continual focus of Aunt Alexandra's attacks, and her aunt's main reason for training Scout to be a lady. A dress will, of course, restrict her activities, leaving the tire rolling and tree climbing as the exclusive domain of the boys. The only time Scout has ever heard Atticus "speak sharply to anyone" was in an altercation with Aunt Alexandra, which "had something to do with my going around in overalls": "Aunt Alexandra was fanatical on the subject of my attire. I could not possibly hope to be a lady if I wore breeches; when I said I could do nothing in a dress, she said I wasn't supposed to be doing things that required pants. Aunt Alexandra's vision of my deportment involved playing with small stoves, tea sets, and wearing the Add-A Pearl necklace she gave me when I was born" (*TKM*, 81).

Later, Aunt Alexandra moves in with them, telling the Finch family that her motive is to provide Scout with "some feminine influence" when the young girl begins to be interested in boys and clothes. Scout remembers: "I could have made several answers to this: Cal's a girl, it would be many years before I would be interested in boys, I would never be interested in clothes" (*TKM*, 127).

"Being a girl" is regarded as so distasteful by the boys with whom she plays that it is not a role that Scout could be encouraged to assume. For example, any reservations she expresses to the boys about the danger in their games elicits taunts of disgust at her "acting like a girl." Even though Aunt Alexandra, a formidable representative of the community, insists that she behave like a girl, she has learned from the boys that "girl" is a term of derision. After Scout refuses to retrieve the tire that has rolled into the Radley yard, Jem says, "'I swear, Scout, sometimes you act so much like a girl it's mortifyin,'" (*TKM*, 38). When, having been frightened by the laugh she alone hears in the Radley house, Scout objects to continuing the Radley drama, Jem accuses her of girlish cowardice: "Jem told me I was being a girl, that girls always imagined things, that's why people hated them so, and if I started behaving like one I could just go off and find some girl to play with" (*TKM*, 41). The language is telling: in Jem's young mind, girls aren't "people" and people hate girls. "On pain of being called a g-irl," she spends less time with the two boys (*TKM*, 42). As she warns the boys against embarking on their mission to peek into the Radley house, Jem says, "I declare to the Lord you're gettin' more like a girl every day!" (*TKM*, 52). Ironically, she herself later equates girlishness with cowardice or squeamishness in thinking of Jem as "girlish" when he forbids her to mash a roly-poly bug.

Yet a girl she is, and everything she despises about the role inflicted on girls, everything that "people" hate about girls is just what she is being pressured to assume. Bewilderingly enough for Scout, when Jem turns twelve, he no longer chides her for acting like a girl. Now he scolds her for not acting like a girl: "'It's time you started bein' a girl and acting right!'" (*TKM*, 115). In the traumatic summer of Tom Robinson's trial, Jem has become more tolerant of Scout as a girl and seems to have come to accept that there are different kinds of girls, and that what is really objectionable to him (but attractive to Aunt Alexandra) is not girls in general but what girls in a particular social caste are forced to become. In comforting Scout after a brush with Aunt Alexandra, he says, "'You know she's not used to girls. . . leastways, not girls like you. She's trying to make you a lady. Can't you take up sewin' or something?'" (*TKM*, 225).

Even worse than being derided as a girl is being excluded as a girl. Her biology reminds Scout of her own ostracism, as when the three children see Mr. Avery urinating off the porch in the moonlight. The boys' discussion of the scene "to determine relative distances and respective prowess only made me feel left out again, as I was untalented in this area" (*TKM*, 51). As the two boys begin serious male bonding during Dill's second summer in Maycomb, Scout seeks out female role models and confidantes, neither of which would meet with Aunt Alexandra's full approval, for one is a black woman, Calpurnia, and the other is Miss Maudie, who also wears men's coveralls during the day and hates to be inside the house. In the same summer that Jem reveals in anger that "people" hate girls, Miss Maudie coolly informs Scout that foot-washing Baptists (like the Radleys, incidentally) "'think that women are a sin by definition'" (*TKM*, 45). Unfortunately, Scout finds that such a view of women is not restricted to foot washers. She has evidently heard the same "Impurity of Women" doctrine from the pulpit of her own church and will hear it again in Cal's black church, leading her to surmise that it "seemed to preoccupy all clergymen." As Calpurnia's minister preaches, "Bootleggers caused enough trouble in the Quarters, but women were worse" (*TKM*, 122).

The boundaries of conventionally perceived gender obviously place Scout in an impossible double bind, for girls and women are reviled by "people," but she must accept that role as well as her identity as a female. And all the restrictions of ladylikeness placed on female behavior, presumably to curb innate depravity, smack of superficiality, oppression, snobbery, and confinement, none of which belong to Scout; those characteristics are, indeed, counter to everything she is and holds dear. Yet those closest to her embrace "feminine" qualities: "Jem had acquired an alien set of values and was trying to impose them on me" (*TKM*, 115).

After the summer when Aunt Alexandra comes to live with them, Scout seems to have accepted the inevitability of being a "lady," of entering "this world, where on its surface fragrant ladies rocked slowly, fanned gently, and drank cool water" (*TKM*, 229). Nevertheless, despite this inevitability, dictated not just by her sex, but particularly by her class, she prefers the male world ("But I was more at home in my father's world" [*TKM*, 233]), because men didn't trick you, and weren't hypocrites.

Gothic Barriers

In examining these superficial trappings of the Gothic, then, there seems to be little doubt that the novel partakes of the Gothic tradition in a significant way. In exploring the internal meanings (as distinct from the external topics) of the Gothic tradition in *TKM*, it is important to realize that the Gothic is fully incorporated into the action, but also parodied in the novel as well.

The internal patterns of the Gothic, especially the modern Gothic, that are also present in *TKM*, include, according to Kate Ferguson Ellis, its social commentary, based upon social and psychological boundaries of every kind. That commentary is intrinsically bound to the tradition's preoccupation at its innermost core with taboos, paranoia, and the barbaric, as David Punter outlines them. Ellis, especially, enlarges on the subject of boundaries and barriers in the Gothic, calling attention to the frequency of forbidding doors, walls, and veils in *TKM*, and providing the reader of the novel with valuable insights into the novel's multiple dimensions. Chief among the Gothic barriers in the novel are the walls of the Radley house, against which Scout rolls in the tire, crashing "into a barrier" (*TKM*, 37); the door of the Dubose house, through which she actually enters the house with her brother Jem, believing that if they go inside they will never emerge again; the door of the Ewell house, which Tom Robinson fearfully and disastrously enters at Mayella's command; the prison fence against which Tom loses his life; the doors of the black church, which are locked to imprison the congregation until they contribute to the collection for Tom's family; the walls of their own house, which protect them from the mad dog who will be shot by their father; the door of the county jail, which Atticus guards; and even the layers of dirt that cover the faces of the despised Ewell children. Finally, we consider the veil of black skin that imprisons many of the town's citizens. Even the community of Maycomb itself is shut off from the rest of the world by boundaries. Scout explains that before Dill joined them and encouraged them to venture out, their summertime boundaries were not objectionable ("We were never tempted to break them" [*TKM*, 11]). Those summertime boundaries, curiously enough, are two hells: the Radley haunted house three doors to the south, and the house of Mrs. Dubose, who was "plain hell," two doors to the north.

Many of the metaphoric walls of the Gothic that lock people in or lock them out are produced by society, a feature of the Gothic that leads Eugenia C. DeLamotte to write: "The Gothic vision has from the beginning been focused steadily on social relations and social institu-tions" (DeLamotte, xii). *TKM* is essentially a social novel, but social in a peculiarly Gothic way, in that it presents a microcosm that focuses the reader on social taboos and social boundaries and emphasizes the tribal nature of the community (DeLamotte, 129). The novel is about the characters in a distinct society and relationship between races and classes. It is within this context that one needs to examine most of the secondary characters who constitute this peculiar community—as peculiar as we might expect any community in any place to appear under scrutiny. Race excluded, this is a Gothic town in which many very eccentric Gothic members of the white population exist under the terms of a not unharmonious truce. The past of the region also makes rigid class distinctions that separate whites of different classes as rigid-ly as they do whites and blacks.

The community the author creates includes five distinct units. One is the landed gentry of Finch's Landing, from which people with two opposite attitudes have arisen: the snobbish, class-conscious Old Southerner, of which Aunt Alexandra is the most notorious represen-tative, and the progressive, intellectual professionals like Atticus, the attorney, and his brother Jack, the physician. The white townspeople of Maycomb form a second group of middle- and upper-class polite society, who are generally somewhat more tolerant in matters of race than their rural neighbors. They are comprised of professionals, busi-nessmen, and retired gentility, who keep themselves as aloof from the Old Sarum poor as they do from the blacks. The rural whites of the country constitute the third and fourth groups, which are made up of the working, uneducated poor, who are warped by hard times and racial prejudice. These characters, the Old Sarum poor, live a marginal existence in the woods. The Finch children and Dill believe that the people of Old Sarum are distinguished from the townspeople by their fiddling and drinking. One group consists of the hard-working, honest poor, many of whom have lost their land during the depression and continue to pay their bills with goods: hickory nuts, holly, turnip greens, and potatoes. The Cunninghams are representative of this group. The children of this Old Sarum group, like Walter Cunningham, have hookworms from wearing no shoes. The fourth unity, an even lower caste in Old Sarum, represented by the Ewells, are mean and shiftless, refuse to send their children to school, hunt out of season, and stay drunk. Unlike the children of the respectable poor in Scout's first grade—Little Chuck Little and Walter Cunningham—the Ewell child, Burris, is "the filthiest human I had ever seen. His neck was dark gray, the backs of his hands were rusty, and his fingernails were black deep into the quick" (*TKM*, 26–27).

Having no whites to look down upon, those whites who live in poverty vent their rage against black men and women who constitute a fifth distinct Maycomb County group. Jem makes another, similar division: "There's four kinds of folks in the world. There's the ordinary kind like us and the neighbors, there's the kind like the Cunninghams out in the woods, the kind like the Ewells down at the dump, and the Negroes" (*TKM*, 226). Each group feels superior to the groups below it in caste, and very infrequently does a member of one group enter the territory of another, and almost never as an equal. As Jem explains to Scout, "The thing about it is, our kind of folks don't like the Cunninghams, the Cunninghams don't like the Ewells, and the Ewells hate and despise colored folks" (*TKM*, 226). Poor whites, the citizens of Old Sarum, traditionally in competition with blacks for jobs, require someone to despise, someone to blame for their plight.

The very concept of social classes arises from those multiple boundaries so important to Gothic fiction and so central to *TKM*. The importance of social class is first impressed on the two Finch children by the arrival of Aunt Alexandra, and later, after the trial so fraught with racial and social tensions, they contemplate what social "quality" means. They discard the idea that it is related to wealth, since in the depression even those with "background" haven't "got a dime to our names." Nor can they believe that upper-class status is conveyed only on "old" families, since "everybody's family's just as old as everybody else's" (*TKM*, 226).

For Jem, the acrimony between social classes is a source of anguish that might explain why Boo Radley sequesters himself in his house: "Why do they go out of their way to despise each other?" he asks (*TKM*, 227).

The community of townspeople comprises a socially homogeneous unit, but one that is made up of very different individuals—all
eccentrics who have reached a truce that allows them to exist harmoniously in fairly close proximity.

They are homogeneous in that they are white, members of the
educated class (Jem is probably not far from correct in supposing that
education makes the crucial difference between white social classes),
and have lived in Maycomb for several generations. One notices, for
example, the isolation and self-sufficiency of Finch's Landing, which
once produced almost everything the family needed. Indeed, those
who live in town and at Finch's Landing are homogeneous to the
extreme, because they have intermarried so much. It is a point that the
narrator makes repeatedly in reference to Atticus's ancestor: "Because
of Simon Finch's industry, Atticus was related by blood or marriage to
nearly every family in town" (*TKM*, 5). In response to Aunt
Alexandra's criticism of "other tribal groups," Jem says, "Aunty better
watch how she talks—scratch most folks in Maycomb and they're kin
to us" (*TKM*, 129). And Atticus, noting Aunt Alexandra's harping on
the unfortunate "streaks" in other people's families—among them,
drinking, gambling, and mean streaks—taunts her with, "Sister, when
you stop to think about it, our generation's practically the first in the
Finch family not to marry its cousins. Would you say the Finches have
an Incestuous Streak?" (*TKM*, 130). "New people," the narrator
observes, "so rarely settled there, the same families married the same
families until the members of the community looked faintly alike"
(*TKM*, 131).

Yet because of this very incestuousness, so characteristic of the
Gothic mode, individuals in town have turned peculiar. Each is an
eccentric character. Among them are the Radleys, who have incarcerated their grown son in the house for years, initially to keep him from
being sent to an industrial school as punishment for being rowdy; Mrs.
Henry Lafayette Dubose, a vicious-tongued old morphine addict; the
amiable Miss Maudie Atkinson, who claims to hate her house, dresses
in men's overalls to tend her beloved plants, sticks her bridgework out
of her mouth to amuse the children, and who shouts defiantly at the
foot-washing Baptists who drive by to condemn her for her too-great

love of the world, that is, her azaleas; Miss Stephanie Crawford, known for doing good and stretching the truth; Mr. Underwood, the newspaper editor who covers the news by looking out the window; and Miss Rachel Haverford, who, since once having found a snake in her closet one morning, always downs a glass of neat whiskey when she arises. Nor is Atticus, himself, mainstream, for he speaks to his children as if they were adults and allows them to address him by his first name.

The townspeople, protected by social barriers from Old Sarum and the black community, are, despite their eccentricities, a tight, cohesive unit who live harmoniously side-by-side, and who join together in most crises, as when Miss Maudie's house burns down. Many of the novel's central scenes occur in centers of social life: the courthouse, the church, and especially the neighborhood street, onto which, from disparate and highly individual private houses, members of the community are drawn in common cause.

The community is also bound by common rituals in attacking common scapegoats. While the townspeople denounce Hitler's use of the Jews as scapegoats, they remain blind to their own use of their black citizenry as scapegoats, their own attacks on and humiliations of a chosen few who fall outside of the pattern of behavior that they have decided to tolerate. Many of their social gatherings involve some manner of violation, to a large or small degree, some kind of group assault. The most ominous ritual is the gathering of the community to witness the trial of Tom Robinson, as if the townspeople mean to involve themselves in the sacrifice of a scapegoat. Much in the description of the atmosphere, which Miss Maudie likens to a "Roman carnival" (*TKM*, 162), is reminiscent of Shirley Jackson's short story, "The Lottery," about the remaining propensity in the twentieth century for the sacrifice of a scapegoat:

> It was like Saturday. People from the south end of the county passed our house in a leisurely but steady stream. . . .A wagonload of ladies rattled past us. They wore cotton sunbonnets and dresses with long sleeves. . . .As the county went by us, Jem gave Dill the histories and general attitudes of the more prominent fig-ures. . . .It was a gala occasion. There was no room at the public

hitching rail for another animal, mules and wagons were parked under every available tree. The courthouse square was covered with picnic parties sitting on newspapers, washing down biscuit and syrup with warm milk from fruit jars.(*TKM*, 158–60)

The community's cohesiveness is like a clannishness, in that it tolerates each of its member's individual rituals. These people make continual compromises to get along with each other. Scout observes "the older citizens, the present generation of people who had lived side by side for years and years were utterly predictable to one another: they took for granted attitudes, character shadings, even gestures, as having been repeated in each generation and refined by time." Thus, certain "dicta" became "simple guides to daily living" (*TKM*, 131).

For example, Dolphus Raymond gives his white neighbors reason to believe that continual, heavy drinking—sipping whiskey from a Coca-cola bottle in a paper sack—causes him to live with black people, rather than inflict his neighbors with the truth—that there is no whiskey in the bottle in the sack and that he'd simply rather associate with blacks than whites. Still another example is Bob Ewell, whose out-of-season hunting the townspeople tolerate because they know that he spends all his money on whiskey, and, but for the game he kills to feed his children, they would go hungry. Calpurnia compromises too, in order to get along in the distinct white and black communities she inhabits. She has one language for use in the Finch house and another for her own people. When the children can't understand why she doesn't talk "right" all the time, she explains her need to compromise:

> "Suppose you and Scout talked colored-folks' talk at home—it'd be out of place, wouldn't it? Now what if I talked white-folks' talk at church, and with my neighbors? They'd think I was puttin' on airs to beat Moses. . . .

> It's not necessary to tell all you know. It's not ladylike—in the second place, folks don't like to have somebody around knowin' more than they do. It aggravates 'em. You're not gonna change any of them by talkin' right, they've got to want to learn themselves, and when they don't want to learn there's nothing you can do but keep your mouth shut or talk their language." (*TKM*, 126)

The rituals of the clan are too bizarre to allow any but the most long-standing resident entry into the mysteries of membership. Outsiders do not find ready admittance, as the new teacher from north Alabama, Miss Caroline Fisher, soon finds out. Scout believes that by simply stating that Walter is a Cunningham, she has provided sufficient explanation to Miss Fisher as to Walter's refusal to borrow a quarter for lunch: "It was clear enough to the rest of us" (*TKM*, 21). Another child, later in the day, also thinks it is a sufficiently clear explanation of Burris Ewell's odd behavior to say, "He's one of the Ewells, ma'am" (*TKM*, 31). Scout wonders "if this explanation would be as unsuccessful as my attempt" (*TKM*, 27). Untaught in the ways of Maycomb, Miss Fisher "makes a serious mistake"—as the other children know—by commanding a Ewell to sit down. Even the young Maycombians know and tolerate, as Miss Fisher does not, that the Cunningham children won't take charity, even if it is a nickel from the teacher for lunch, and that the Ewell children attend school for only the first day of the year.

TABOOS, PARANOIA, AND VIOLENCE

The society of *TKM* is formed, then, by the very forces that traditionally have characterized Gothic fiction: fear-inspiring taboos, paranoia, and fear of the barbaric, all of which, in themselves, are founded on rigid boundaries. David Punter describes taboo as "that pleasure which is felt when meddling with components of life which are outside the pale of 'civilized discourse'" (Punter, 410), and that have reference to those areas of life "which offend, which are suppressed, which are generally swept under the carpet in the interests of social and psychological equilibrium" (Punter, 405). The taboos of the novel include miscegenation, incest, various kinds of interaction between different segments of white society, and behavioral taboos that help define and protect social groups. Thus, taboos raise boundaries that are both protectively good and confiningly bad. The children themselves find pleasure in the prospect of defying certain taboos, as when Scout tries to violate the convention that prohibits a white child from visiting in a black household. Mayella Ewell moves from one taboo, incest, to another, miscegenation. Indeed, her attraction to Tom Robinson is the opposite of incest. The latter, though taboo, is the ultimate self-enclosure, the destructive eating away of self in confinement, as we find in Edgar Allan Poe's "The Fall of the House of Usher." Mayella's attraction to Tom, the opposite of herself in every way, is, ironically, a more healthy impulse to join with the outside world.

Paranoia results when, according to Punter, "the reader is placed in a situation of ambiguity with regard to fears within the text" (Punter, 404), as when in *TKM*, the reader, empathizing with the characters, must sort out the racial fears of the white community and the children's fears of the supernatural. Paranoia serves to raise and preserve and also to resist social boundaries, threatening to set in when one group makes a move to violate social boundaries.

The trial of a black man, charged by a Ewell who lives at the dump, defended by a lawyer from the town, and judged by a jury made up of the more respectable poor, like the Cunninghams, creates a particularly complex dynamic, in which members of every class are forced into the traumatic ritual of interaction. Much of the critical action occurs in scenes of disruption, when a member of one class makes an incursion into the forbidden territory of another: the Ewells create havoc in coming to the town's school, even though it is only for one day of the year; a poor Cunningham child disrupts lunch in the house of the lawyer and his family; a confrontation occurs in a black church when the white children appear for services, with a church member saying to Calpurnia, "You ain't got no business bringin' white chillun here—they got their church, we got our'n" (*TKM*, 119); an ugly scene unfolds when a group of Old Sarum residents come to town at night; discord is the result when a Finch's Landing resident, Aunt Alexandra, moves into the house of Atticus and his children, and when Atticus's family visits Finch's Landing at Christmas. The most destructive disruption occurs when Mayella Ewell asks a black man, Tom Robinson, to first come inside the Ewell fence and then the Ewell house.

The glue of the community is not only common blood but a common ground and a shared past: a Civil War and the subsequent isolation and suffering, as well as lingering attitudes toward class and race, with their roots in the plantation system. According to David Punter, the Gothic shows the immense power exerted by the ideology of the established society to make its version of the world, in which the establishment has a stake, seem natural and stable, even if the society supported by the ideology is divided by grotesque social, racial, and sexual boundaries: "The fact that bourgeois ideology can naturalize this unstable situation [of a changeless society] sufficiently well to keep the state in operation does not mean that the contradictions and falsities underneath will not surface" (Punter, 425). And surface they do in *TKM*. Maycomb's citizens may have reached a truce, but Maycomb, for all its individual compromises in the interests of peace and stability, is a community whose violence lies just barely beneath the surface. Kate Ferguson Ellis writes of the Gothic that "forces of violence are generated by an anxiety about boundaries: those that shut the protagonist off from the world, those that shut the protagonist in, and those that separate the individual self from something that is Other" (Ellis, 19).

Even the civilized Finch family has in its history a notorious episode of madness and violence. Atticus's cousin (who, as Aunt Alexandra is proud to point out, wrote a book with the unlikely religious title *Meditations of Joshua S. St. Clair*), while a student at the University of Alabama, tried to shoot the university president with a gun that finally blew up in his hand (*TKM*, 132).

Scout's own violence seems prompted by her resistance to the barriers of gender, to being locked in to the submissive, genteel behavior expected of "a girl" or "a young lady." Exhibiting the audacious violence of a child, on numerous occasions she lights into other children with her fists, beginning in the first grade with Walter Ewell, who, inadvertently and just by his very presence, was the cause of Scout's punishment by the teacher: "Catching Walter Cunningham in the schoolyard gave me some pleasure, but when I was rubbing his nose in the dirt Jem came by and told me to stop. 'You're bigger'n he is,' he said" (*TKM*, 22). At Christmastime, she attacks her cousin Francis: "This time, I split my knuckle to the bone on his front teeth. My left impaired, I sailed in with my right" (*TKM*, 84).

Even among the first grade children, there is the threat of a kind of violence that forebodes ugliness—a kind that one suspects will never be tamed or civilized. When one of the Old Sarum Ewell children menaces the teacher, the scene is fraught with violence on the part of her attacker and her protector, giving Miss Foster a crash course in this south Alabama community:

> Little Chuck Little got to his feet. "Let him go, ma'am," he said. "He's a mean one, a hard-down mean one. He's liable to start somethin', and there's some little folks here."
>
> He was among the most diminutive of men, but when Burris Ewell turned toward him, Little Chuck's right hand went to his pocket. "Watch your step, Burris," he said. "I'd soon's kill you as look at you. Now go home." (*TKM*, 27–28)

Old Sarum, the home of Little Chuck Little and Burris Ewell and Walter Cunningham, is a place where violence always threatens to spill over into the more restrained town of Maycomb. Old Sarum's violence is self-contained most of the time, as for a time in the Ewell household, where the children are abused by a drunken bully, their father. Sometimes, however, violence invades the town, as when the mob from Old Sarum threatens to lynch Tom Robinson, or when Bob Ewell descends on the town seeking retribution for the alleged rape of his daughter by Tom.

So, in the Gothic tradition, social taboos and paranoia generate and are generated by established ideology, creating an uneasy and superficial tranquility beneath and against which violence constantly threatens to erupt. Boundaries, paranoia, and taboo are also erected from the Gothic fear of the barbaric, a fear that is evident in the town's apprehension that what they see as barbaric in Old Sarum and the black community will rise up to break down the protective walls around "polite" society. The fear of the barbaric is also apparent in the children's fear of and attraction to something primordially supernatural on the other side of the protective wall of civilized rationality. The classic example is the children's paranoia over Boo Radley, along with their fear that ghosts and vampires will not remain confined to the spirit world of the dead, but will pass through protective barriers to mix with the living.

Parody, Romance, and Terror

Yet, for all the trappings of the Gothic and the novel's participation in the Gothic tradition of boundaries, it is also a parody of the Gothic vision, a characteristic that also, ironically, marks the traditional Gothic itself. William Patrick Day, in his study of the Gothic, emphasizes that it operates as a parody of other narratives and conceptions of the world (Day, 4). According to Day, the Gothic subverts, therefore parodies, literary forms that proclaim systematic visions of the wholeness and unity of the world and the self. In *TKM*, the Gothic as an exaggeration is represented through the imaginations of the children, who view Boo Radley as one of the walking dead, and whose pecan trees, they are sure, bear lethal fruit. The parody of the Gothic is accomplished by a contrasting the world as the children perceive it— gothically constructed of dark secrets and evil spirits—with the naturalistic world, which contains more evil and darkness than they possibly could have encountered supernaturally. As Day writes, the supernatural and monstrous are illusions in many Gothic novels, and that "it is the impression of strangeness, the sensation that one is in the presence of that which suspends and calls into doubt the laws of the universe that is essential to the Gothic, even if this effect is later explained away" (Day, 35). Just so, although the children come to drop their stereotyped view of Boo Radley as monstrous, their childhood has been influenced by their conviction that the laws of the universe have been suspended in supernatural terror.

Though the Gothic is largely an antirealistic mode, the realism of *TKM* is still within the Gothic tradition as David Punter explains it. One view taken in the Gothic is that the world is largely as realists see it, but that there are "moments when it is quite different, and that these moments are of peculiar, epiphanic importance" (Punter, 406). A second kind of Gothic text shows that the world only looks real "from an established (dominant, bourgeois) viewpoint"; other views show it to be quite different (Punter, 407). A third approach, in the tradition of Poe, Melville, and Hawthorne, makes the case that the world is not at all as the realists see it. And yet another kind of Gothic argues that while the world is real on the surface, underneath there is something else—in short, a divided world. Finally, there is the view that there is no world at all, only our fictions.

In a sense, *TKM* encompasses all five approaches to reality. In the world of the novel, which is basically realistic, there is an undeniable element of magic about Boo Radley's uncanny knowledge of the children and his ability to save them; and an ominous, monstrous evil about Bob Ewell that emanates from a level beneath reality. As to Punter's second point, one might argue that what is real is only a matter of perspective, the establishment's view being only one of many. The children's perspective is much like Poe's: the world is not at all like realists describe it. Perhaps, the novel suggests, there is no world, only perspectives of it, only the fiction or fictions. After all, the establishment has described the "real" character of the African-American, which is unveiled as a societal fiction in the novel. Society has determined what the reality of femaleness is, and it is certainly not true of Scout's "unladylike" nature. Is society's version of reality any less true than the children's versions? or the author's?

William Patrick Day's argument in *In the Circles of Fear and Desire* is that, while the Gothic is an offshoot of Romanticism in its failure to affirm reality as Truth, its fantasy is "based on a conception directly opposed to the romantic vision of the transcendent power and energy of the imagination." Day contends that "a central fact about the genre, is the announcement of its own discontinuity with the real world; it always makes its own artificiality and fictiveness clear. It represents a world that does not in fact exist" (Day, 13). In Romanticism, the typical hero or heroine slips from a higher to a lower world, "from the Edenic or natural world to the underworld, in search of lost identity" (Day, 7), to ascend to some kind of wholeness. In the Gothic, while the hero or heroine enters an underworld as in the romance, Day argues that he or she doesn't regain a wholeness of identity, but instead becomes locked in a fragmented chaos of an underworld where transformations never cease and where the monstrous becomes "the shadow and mockery of the human" (Day, 8). While unrelieved monstrousness characterizes the children's stereotypes of Arthur Radley and Mrs. Dubose, for example, they themselves appear to escape the

Gothic chaos of self in rising from an underworld of fear to a wholeness of vision.

References to literature set up the tension in the novel between a dark reality and romance, both of which are regarded as elements of the Gothic. While the children love romance and tend at first to romanticize their night stalkers, their romanticism is somewhat leavened by the reality they find through their customary reading of the daily newspapers. Furthermore, they are not such indiscriminate slaves to romance that they cannot and do not reject certain kinds of romance; rather, romance seems to have to have that dark and evil edge for them to accept it. Scout loves Tom Swift and Tarzan, but, like her classmates who are "immune to imaginative literature," she is unwilling to swallow the stories read by her first grade teacher, Miss Caroline Fisher, about toads living in halls and talking cats in "cunning" clothes (*TKM*, 16).

The malignancy of romance is most apparent in the association of Sir Walter Scott's *Ivanhoe*, a novel synonymous with romance, with Mrs. Dubose, the repugnant old woman to whom Jem must read the novel as she withdraws from morphine.

The discussion of the Gothic in *TKM* cannot be closed without some consideration of the eternal question of the lure of terror: It is always a matter of curiosity that some people—especially some children—relish being scared. Perhaps much of it has to do with the fact that being scared makes them feel more alive. Ironically, brushes with death, even in literature, seem to heighten the spirit, as Edgar Allan Poe believed and as Sigmund Freud explained in "The Uncanny." According to Poe, terror was the effect most likely to bring about a kind of transcendence, to afford one a glimpse or a feeling of supernatural beauty—that realm of absolute truth for which we yearn but rarely are able to see.

Another characteristic of the Gothic is summed up by Kate Ferguson Ellis when she writes, "Not knowing is the primary source of Gothic terror" (Ellis, 24). And we are drawn to terror in part because through it we can experience the unknown. What heightens Boo Radley's ability to inspire terror as well as the children's attraction to his house is that they have never seen him, though he lives so close to them, and they have no convincing explanation for the horrors in the Radley house. Boo's assault on his father, to which they return repeatedly, is especially frightening because it cannot be explained. There appears to be no immediate motive for the attack, nor any explanatory rage. Miss Stephanie's account, calculated no doubt for a full effect of fright, emphasizes the mindlessness of the assault: "As Mr. Radley passed by his son in the living room, Boo drove the scissors into his parent's leg, pulled them out, wiped them on his pants, and resumed his activities" (*TKM*, 11).

6

The Danger and Delight of Difference

A consideration of the Gothic elements in *To Kill a Mockingbird*—particularly its use of the supernatural and its preoccupation with boundaries—directs discussion to a consideration of one of the predominant themes of the novel, the attraction to and the encounter with the Other. Kate Ferguson Ellis sees the concept of the Other as central to the Gothic as she writes that, in the Gothic, anxiety arises about barriers "that separate the individual self from something that is Other" (Ellis, 19), adding that "two fears dominate this Gothic world, the fear of terrible separateness and the fear of unity with some terrible Other" (Ellis, 22). Rosemary Jackson also argues that the Gothic has to do with our discovery of the Other hidden in the self. The abiding presence of the Other is central to William Patrick Day's exploration of the Gothic. He writes that in discussing atmosphere in the Gothic, we are led to "the nature of a world that is 'not-self,' or 'Other,' and that in discussing conventions of plot in the Gothic, we are led to an exploration of "the nature of the relationship of self to Other" (Day, 15). He further writes, "The relationship between self and Other is defined by the struggle between the impulse to domination and the impulse to submission. . . .The [Gothic] fantasy defines its world as Other" and "the Other resolves itself into a version of the self," leading to "the transformation and metamorphosis of the self into its opposite, either into the Other or its own hidden double. . . .the self is found in the Other, and the Other is in fact a face of the self" (Day, 19–22). Day defines the true Gothic as the fear (and desire) that the barrier between the self and the Other will be broken: "The true terror lies in the possibility that the Gothic atmosphere will take over completely and that the conventional, stable division between self and Other will disappear forever" (Day, 27). In *TKM*, this is illustrated most plainly in the Maycomb community's demonization of the black man as the Other and in the community's terror of the boundaries between self (the whites) and Other (the blacks) being erased in that worst of all occurrences, miscegenation.

The concept of an "Other" has both psychological and sociological meanings, neither of which is entirely exclusive of the other approach. Psychological enlargement of the idea is generally connected with the work of Jacques Lacan, and the sociological with writers on gender, race, and culture, such as Simone de Beauvoir, Frantz Fanon, and Edward Said. Lacan defines the Other as the not-Me, referring to "the various external forces that structure a primary and secondary unconscious"[1] that are basically alien to the subject; Lacan also asserts that "people constitute each other Imaginarily as objects in an ongoing effort or 'impulse' to verify their own identities retroactively in terms of sameness and difference" (Lacan, 15–16).

TKM invites the conclusion that we reach some sense of self-identity by our encounters with other forces, that is, with forces alien to our commonplace lives. As a result of these encounters, we break the cultural and psychological barriers that imprison us and come to embrace a larger world. At the same time, we also recognize and embrace a heretofore unknown, usually darker quality within ourselves—the Other within our own skin. Atticus will say repeatedly that you can never understand a person "until you climb into his skin and walk around in it" (*TKM*, 30), and Scout, following his advice, will try "to climb into Jem's skin and walk around in it" in order to understand her brother (*TKM*, 57). Through such encounters, as playwright Arthur Miller writes in *After the Fall*, we learn to embrace not only the

Other, the Different One, outside ourselves, but the monstrosity to which it corresponds within ourselves. The horror no longer terrifies us. Instead, it becomes familiar, and through our experience we are joined with rather than terrified by the world in all its dark complexity. The Other—any entity, markedly different from the sheltered self—can conceivably take many forms. In its most extreme manifestation, it is a literal alien from outer space—it is Count Dracula, or Frankenstein's monster; it is a witch, or a madman, both initially appearing as contrasts to the supposedly sane and innocent self, far removed from the defining social strictures of one's own narrow world; it is most often perceived in a person of another race.

The theme of the Other is especially strong in a community that is described as being homogeneous to the point of intermarriage, for the dark Unlike is more pronounced than usual in a town where most of the people in "acceptable" society are virtually alike. In *TKM*, the Other manifests itself primarily in that creature of the night, Boo Radley, a man kept completely isolated in his father's house from his youth onward. The children see their encounter with Boo as a turning point in their lives. For example, as the children, now grown, discuss the story that the narrator unfolds, we learn that Jem believes all the events that led to his injury at the novel's close "began the summer Dill came to us, when Dill first gave us the idea of making Boo Radley come out" (*TKM*, 3). Boo is unseen and unknown. He is the chief character in a village story that has become myth, comprised of a psychologically stunted man who in one brief moment of madness stabs his father in the leg with scissors.

What makes Boo so horrible is not only the story of this one insane act, but his utter unknowability, his complete removal from society, and the fact that he is perceived as being everything that the children are not. He is shut in the house during the day while the children play in the yard, and wanders outside at night while they gather around their father inside the house and then go to sleep. Further, the Radley family is strange and unknown; the house's doors are closed, while the Finches and their neighbors leave their doors open. The Radleys never emerge on Sundays, when the townspeople gather in churches and pay calls on one another in the afternoon.

The Vampire

One of the most conspicuous Gothic references in the novel is to Count Dracula, a legend that functions as a representation of the Other, who is so unlike the ordinary self in his supernatural creature-hood, hovering in the territory between life and death. What heightens our horror at his blood-sucking power over others is our uncertainty about how to classify him—is he living or dead?—and our uncertainty about our own reactions to him: We are both drawn to and frightened by him. The demonic nature of his Otherness is heightened by our sense that he has not only broken a taboo in his habit of consuming human blood, but that his very existence, in failing to yield to easy categorization, upsets our confidence in Nature's order and resists or defies lawfulness and certainties.

The references to Count Dracula in the novel are significant, and begin with the younger Finches' first conversation with Dill: "Dill had seen Dracula, a revelation that moved Jem to eye him with the beginning of respect. 'Tell it to us,' he said. . . .Dill reduced Dracula to dust, and Jem said the show sounded better than the book" (*TKM*, 7–8). This conversation occurs only several lines before we learn of Dill's fascination with Boo Radley, and certainly Boo has vampirelike characteristics in the children's minds. Like a vampire, he is a night walker, a shape shifter, the boy with fangs who eats raw squirrels, the recluse who has, as Atticus says, been turned into a ghost. Both the horror and the attraction of the Other that is Boo Radley is intensified in the children's association of him with the devil, also a vampirish figure.

Criticism that searches out the universal meanings of the Dracula legend is useful in pursuing the theme of engagement with the Other, especially as it focuses on Boo Radley in *TKM*. Count Dracula's story takes on a frequent Gothic theme, transformation, in its story of the unnatural power of the devil's avatar over the lives of others. Dracula, in all his nighttime luridness, is the extreme demonic Other, frightening in his degree of difference from the everyday self. Furthermore, he is an inversion of Christian conversion. That is, he has been converted by the devil to eternal death in life rather than to eternal life in death. In *TKM*, however, the vampirish monstrosity of Boo Radley has been created, in Frankenstein-like fashion, by the children (with undeniable assistance from Arthur Radley's family). The children, initially, and much of the community, project onto Arthur Radley dark satanic powers that are foreign to their ordinary lives, not realizing that they share a similar darkness, manifested in their urge to hurt and to control by force.

But there is a twist in this novel, for *TKM* is the classic story of a countertransformation of the Dracula legend, for the children find that the monstrosity—the Antichrist—of their own making has become transformed into the familiar. Moreover, he has become a guardian angel—a savior.

Essentially, the terror of Count Dracula is his embodiment of death in life, as is the case with the ghosts, which the children call "Hot Steams." They are, as William Patrick Day notes, death incarnate, all visitors to this world from the land of the dead, the Other side. It is significant that the first discussion the children have about "Hot Steams" or ghosts takes place as they are staring at the Radley house. At the same time that the children pretend it is beneath them to believe in "Hot Steams," they are riveted by the idea of them, not just as scary phenomena from which they have to protect themselves with magical chants, but as a possible condition to which they themselves might be damned. As Jem explains: "'If you walk through him, when you die you'll be one too, an you'll go around at night suckin' people's breath'" (*TKM*, 37).

THE WITCH

As was done in New England towns almost three hundred years earlier, Maycomb also has turned Arthur Boo Radley into another threatening and horrific Other—the witch. For centuries, whole communities persecuted supposed witches as demonic Others in the same way that much of Maycomb and the novel's three children project witchhood onto Arthur Radley. And, in fact, Boo has several significant characteristics of the classic witch. He is something of a dark mystery in the community; he is a recluse, living completely shut away from ordinary people; he and his family are frightening in their eccentricities—Arthur is even believed to be a dangerous lunatic; he has been the perpetrator of an assault on his father and is believed to commit petty crimes and feats of black magic, becoming for all intents and purposes the community scapegoat: supposedly, he not only peeps in windows, but he mutilates pets, poisons trees and kills flowering shrubs.

More than this, Boo lives in an evil and sentient witch house. While it is the house itself that has made Boo Radley a horror, the children seem to perceive it the other way around. The shingles are rotten and falling off; the once-white paint has worn off or turned dark; the fence is ragged and surrounds a yard in perpetual shade. With its yard harboring no grass and the house itself in disrepair, Boo's frightening abode is the only physical evidence the children have of his own character. It is a house that the narrator describes as having died (*TKM*, 12).

To this Other the children are inevitably and unceasingly drawn, their potent imaginations propelling them toward Boo more intensely with every revelation of horror. The essential thrust of the narrative is the children's attempt to get closer to the horror, to approach the Other, which is so mysterious, so unlike what they know of themselves and their own lives.

The vampirish, ghostlike quality of the Other is frequently linked to death, and especially, to the intrusion of death in life. Its accompanying violence plays an integral part in the children's encounter with the darkness that lies beneath the surface of their sunny, languid, small-town reality. The resolution of three of the important plots and subplots of the novel end in deaths—two of them unmistakably violent and one grotesque. None of the three seems entirely natural. The first is the hard death of Mrs. Dubose, after she suffers great pain from her physical ailments. The second is the violent death of Tom Robinson, who is shot repeatedly in a prison yard. And the third is the stabbing death of Bob Ewell by Boo Radley.

On another level, the children's obsession with death invades life, as seen in their beliefs in the walking dead, like vampires and ghosts (the Hot Steams), and in the ghost or vampire they first perceive Boo Radley to be.

In contrast to the violent and untimely deaths in the novel, and the death-in-life and live burials, the First Purchase African M.E. Church graveyard is a happy cemetery, where death is a natural part of the cycle of life (although there is the acknowledgment that some dead, who have lightning rods placed on their graves, rest uneasily).

PLAY AND RITUAL

Continually, we see that the children, in true Gothic fashion, view the Other with both fear and desire (Day, 23). They initially approach Boo Radley, in their first summer with Dill, by merely gazing on his house steadfastly. So enthralled are they with the Other, that they display another characteristic of the Gothic—voyeurism, in the tradition of Robert Louis Stevenson's Henry Jekyll and Nathaniel Hawthorne's Miles Coverdale. But the voyeurism of the novel crosses back and forth from the children to the Other: the children attempt to peep at Arthur Radley through the window; Dill gazes constantly at the Radley house; Boo is rumored to have looked into Miss Stephanie Crawford's window; and we come to realize at the novel's close that Boo has watched the children as closely as they have tried to watch him. There are other obvious and implied examples of voyeurism in the novel, as, for example, when the crowd outside the courtroom watches Dolphus Raymond; when we come to believe that Mayella Ewell watches Tom from her house; when the courtroom crowd, with a measure of prurient curiosity, watches the trial; when the children watch Mr. Avery urinating under cover of darkness. The meaning of this voyeurism is explained by William Patrick Day: "The act of observing another person, often, though not always, secretly, is a paradigmatic Gothic motif; it is the act of watching one's self. . . .The object of the voyeur's attention is a mirror of the self" (Day, 64–65).

The course of the children's engagement with Boo Radley begins with Dill. The narrator recalls, "The more we told Dill about the Radleys, the more he wanted to know, the longer he would stand hugging the light-pole on the corner, the more he would wonder" (*TKM*,

12). This is followed by Jem's race, on a dare, into the Radley yard to touch the house and to race back out, after which the children think they see "a tiny, almost invisible movement" at the window (*TKM*, 15). During the school year, Boo, having been approached, makes the next move. He hides things for the children in the hole of an oak tree on the Radley property. At first, what they receive is no more than chewing gum. They suspect, since it comes from so near the witch's house, that it might be poisonous. But the growing familiarity with something once so dreaded and different, as well as a measure of childhood greed and foolhardiness, lead them to place the gift in their mouths. They seem to feel, but cannot fully accept, that this white magic comes from Arthur Boo Radley. The gifts that follow confirm their notion that a mysterious, almost supernatural being has placed things in the tree for them. After the chewing gum they find Indian-head pennies in a ring box. These, Jem tells Scout, are a source of "real strong magic" (*TKM*, 35).

In the second summer, it is Scout who has the close encounter with the Radley house, when a tire in which she is riding goes astray and rolls against the steps of the dreaded witch house. This, her own contact with the Other, seems too frightening, even sacred, to utter. She fails to tell the two boys that while she was lying dazed on the ground in the Radley yard that she heard laughter coming from within the house.

It is also during this summer that the children accustom themselves to the terror by playing out the drama of the Radley family, taking the roles of Boo and his parents, thus perversely doing what Atticus has always taught them they should do: understand people different from themselves by walking around in their shoes or "skins." The word "skin" is suggestive here because it conjures up primitive, ritual shamans who wrapped themselves in the skins of the animals they hoped to subdue or appease. Just as humans have played out, since the beginning of time, tales of the unknowable and inexplicable, so do the three children, recapitulating the actions of people of earlier cultures, who took on the roles, that is the identities, of gods and spirits, heroes and villains, and used ritual, played out in slightly different ways day after day, to come to terms with something fearful. Jem's and Scout's and Dill's childish art, that is, their dramatic ritual, is an early step in a very elemental, universal process of taming the darkness while at the same time recognizing one's kinship with it. For Jem, especially, the Radley drama is a repetitive rite of passage from childhood to adolescence.

Anthropological and psychological studies of ritual and play bear out the children's journey together, as Scout calls it, especially the somewhat ceremonial performance of the Radley drama, as a means of exploring the world and the self, for such studies tell us that play and rituals, usually associated with myth, mark critical events in the life of individuals: rites of passage; social changes; and separation from the former self, the separation from childhood dramatized by a simulation of death, which often involves some kind of bodily alteration. Ancient dramas were designed to restore equilibrium, according to some anthropologists.[2] D. W. Winnicott writes in *Playing and Reality* that, "It is in playing and only in playing that the individual child or adult is able to create and to use the whole personality, and it is only in being creative that the individual discovers the self."[3] Freudian psychologist Rosemary Gould also sees the imaginative play of very young children as steps in self-definition, because they take the roles of protector or villain or aggressor.[4]

Children's self-definition through drama and play has been found to be an expression of social conflict as often as it is an expression of social cohesion. For example, Helen B. Schwartzman notes that certain children's games actually challenge social order, in that they reverse or mock authoritative and submissive social roles. She contends that play does not just preserve past social or cultural order. Rather it transforms it, often becoming antiauthoritarian in its challenge of the status quo.[5] In the case of Dill and the Finch children, they repeat their community's story of irrationality and disorder. That is the story they choose, the story that impels them. At the same time, their play undermines the authority of the father figure by making heroic the seemingly villainous and irrational father-attacker, Arthur Radley, thereby turning community lore into a myth about the hero's exploits in defiance of the meanest man in the world, as Calpurnia calls the Radley patriarch. The plays of order and disorder are ways of either adapting to the community or preparing for cultural change by experimenting with several different roles, acting out dramas from real life to "master" them, or to project their fears onto the characters they play (Schwartzman, 145).

Children's dramas are interpretations not only of the roles they are playing, but also of their own real-life situations, and therefore reflect their own status. So we learn that Scout is usually relegated to less-important roles when her only playmate is her older brother. For a time, Dill, as a newcomer, must take on some of the undesirable roles once given to Scout. Once Dill establishes himself as a member of the little group, however, and bonds with Jem as a male, he moves into better roles: "He was clearly tired of being our character man" (*TKM*, 36). Scout, as a girl and as the youngest of the three, protests that she must again return to the least interesting parts: "'I'm tired of those,' I said. I was tired of playing Tom Rover, who suddenly lost his memory in the middle of a picture show and was out of the script until the end, when he was found in Alaska" (*TKM*, 36). By the time the children are acting out the Radley drama, Scout sees that she is clearly getting the leftover parts, and the boys finally throw her a sop in the part of the probate judge who sentences Boo. As Schwartzman sums up this pattern:

> By providing children with an opportunity for commentary or interpretation, play suggests the possibility of reinterpretation, challenge, and even change in relationships. Make-believe play creates these possibilities because it is both text and context. This, then, is the beginning of humor, art, and all forms of social satire and critique and is perhaps the most significant feature of this play form. . . .But play is also productive in other ways; most especially it gives shape (i.e., it generates) and also gives expression to a child's developing emotional-social and cognitive systems. Children at play learn how to be sensitive to the effects of context and the importance of relationships; they develop the capacity to adopt an "as if" set toward objects, actions, persons, and situations; and they continually explore the possibilities of interpretation and reinterpretation and within this the creation of new possibilities. (Schwartzman, 245, 328)

As was already mentioned, Atticus has always taught Jem and Scout to walk around in the shoes of others in order to understand them, and without realizing it, this is exactly what the children are doing when they act out the Tom Swift, the Dracula, the Tarzan, and the Radley stories. The children do, admittedly, fashion the monstrous according to their own inclinations. In so doing, they make the unknown even more frightening than it really is, as if, ironically, to make the impact of these horrors on their hearts more immediate, more felt. At the same time, however, they are not only drawing closer to making friends with those horrors so alien to themselves, but are also dramatically identifying with and melding with the forces of darkness, and thereby drawing on their own darkness, bringing it closer to the surface in safe, literary ways. In their first summer together, the children continue the dramas that have already been a part of the play of Jem and Scout, adding an actor and a new dimension as Dill becomes a participant. By the end of the first summer, their dramatic productions have become "countless reproductions" of stories from Tarzan, the Rover Boys, and Tom Swift. On the first day of the second summer with Dill, their dramas commence again, but this time with a more direct connection to darkness and difference, as they refashion and enact over and over again the saga of the Radleys, which according to Jem is "'something new, something different'" (*TKM*, 38).

That the front yard playacting, in which they will re-create the Radley story, has immense significance for the children and the narrative is suggested by the fact that the endeavor is so frightening, it takes courage to assume the roles. Jem "had thought that up [the idea of the Radley drama] to make me understand he wasn't afraid of Radleys in any shape or form, to contrast his own fearless heroism with my cowardice" (*TKM*, 38). It is automatically assumed, and rightly so, that Scout is afraid to take part in the drama: "'Smatter?' said Dill. 'Still scared?'" and "'Jem, you and me can play and Scout can watch if she's scared'" (*TKM*, 39). Scout is scared, and she agrees reluctantly to take part in the Radley dramas only to prove her bravery: "I played that summer with more than vague anxiety despite Jem's assurances that Boo Radley was dead and nothing would get me" (*TKM*, 39).

The Radley drama is the children's ritual throughout the summer: "We polished and perfected it, added dialogue and plot until we had manufactured a small play upon which we rang changes every day"

(*TKM*, 39). They also add further horror to the Radley myth: Boo, Dill decides, bit off his mother's finger one night, "when he couldn't find any cats and squirrels to eat" (*TKM*, 39). In light of the Radley dramas as an enactment of the sensational and unfamiliar, two interesting details emerge from the descriptions of the children's play. First, the narrator reveals that Scout's view of the drama as dangerous arises from the fact that she, unlike Jem and Dill, has proof of Boo's existence: She heard him laugh behind the door when she rolled up against the Radley porch in the tire. Second, the description of their play seems to suggest that Boo was the hero of the dramas. The narrator recalls that "Jem, naturally, was Boo," and a few lines later, that "Jem was a born hero" (*TKM*, 39). Both details suggest that the children are at two different stages in their approach to the dark Other. Jem and Dill are still in the earliest stage of regarding the dark Other as a figure of romance. Boo, as well as Dracula, has been fictionalized, almost idealized. On the other hand, Scout, at this point, has been brought farther into dark and fearful reality in having actually heard the demon laugh.

There is another element in the dramas that parallels primitive ritual: what the children are literally playing out is the ancient story of the death of the patriarch, whose son can then take his father's place as a man. The main action of the drama, and what the children repeatedly enact throughout the summer, having made the son the hero, is Boo's attack on his father. Any resentment of Atticus that Jem and Scout feel at this point in their lives is decidedly sublimated, but present nevertheless. They do have their minor complaints about his age and unwillingness to play with them in the way that other fathers do with their children, and they have not yet had the revelation that he is a dead shot. Atticus never did "anything that could possibly arouse the admiration of anyone," Scout thinks (*TKM*, 89). The news that Atticus can play a Jew's harp only "served to make me even more ashamed of him" (*TKM*, 91). Miss Maudie will remind Scout after the shooting of the mad dog, "Still think your father can't do anything? Still ashamed of him?" (*TKM*, 98). Yet, unlike Dill, who may well feel personally resentful toward his neglectful father, Scout's and Jem's rebellion, played out in the dramas, is more against what generic Father represents, that is, the oppressiveness of the established order, which Scout comes up against with a vengeance upon entering first grade. In light of this view of the ritual, it is interesting that it is Atticus who calls a halt to the little drama.

TRANSFORMATION

That same summer, the children attempt to give Boo a letter by leaving it on a windowsill. The summer ends on the evening before Dill leaves, when the children risk getting shot by Mr. Radley for peeping through the Radley's window to try to get a glimpse of the monster. After quickly fleeing, Jem creeps back to retrieve his trousers from the Radley's barbed wire fence, only to find them crudely mended and neatly folded and waiting for him. Just as the children had tried to enter the horror through their play, the horror had entered Jem's mind: "Like somebody was readin' my mind. . .like somebody could tell what I was gonna do. Can't anybody tell what I'm gonna do lest they know me, can they Scout?" (*TKM*, 58).

Throughout the winter, the children maintain guarded communication with the strangeness. They relish the chewing gum they find in the oak tree, "the fact that everything on the Radley Place was poison having slipped Jem's memory" (*TKM*, 60). They find string, and then another witch's apparatus—two figures, puppets, carved from soap. That these are understood to be witch's poppets is made plain in Scout's reaction to them: "Before I remembered that there was no such thing as hoo-dooing, I shrieked and threw them down" (*TKM*, 59). This is positive proof to the reader as to the gifts' source, though the children still do not seem ready to acknowledge that Boo, their witch-like neighbor, is watching them as surely as they are trying to know him. After first recovering an old spelling medal and a watch and chain from the tree, their attempts at further communication are thwarted when they find the hole in the "perfectly healthy" tree cemented over (*TKM*, 63).

It is in November, on the night when Miss Maudie's house catches fire, that they have the closest encounter with the unknown in the person of Boo Radley, and confirm what they have long suspected—that his is white instead of black magic. Scout realizes this as she stands on the Radley porch near his window at the novel's end, having seen him into the house, and now watches the street as he would have seen it over the past several years: "Summer, and he watched his children's heart break. Autumn again, and Boo's children needed him" (*TKM*, 279). It is not until the children are back home after having watched the conflagration all night that they realize that Boo slipped a blanket around Scout's shoulders in the freezing night air. It is the first of two recognition scenes for Scout, both involving Boo. She begins to know fully who has been communicating with them in the tree, and who gave her the blanket, and she is enlightened by Jem's changed view of their strange neighbor: "He's crazy, I reckon, like they say, but Atticus, I swear to God he ain't ever harmed us, he ain't ever hurt us, he coulda cut my throat from ear to ear that night but he tried to mend my pants instead. . .he ain't ever hurt us, Atticus" (*TKM*, 72). Boo, who had been the threatening ghost, the witching wizard, the vampire in service of the devil, has turned into a guardian angel.

The ultimate confrontation of the dark Other in the form of Boo Radley occurs, appropriately, on Halloween night, a time "when the souls of the departed were supposed to revisit" the earth, when witches sped "on their errands of mischief," and "hobgoblins of every sort roamed freely about."[6] The ritual of the children's Radley play is recapitulated on Halloween night, as Scout, at least, again appears in a drama in a guise. The Halloween drama of the history of Maycomb, with its actors costumed as "agricultural products"—Scout herself as a ham—is Maycomb's version of an ancient harvest festival. The events of the entire evening embody the elements of the death and resurrection, not only of the harvest festival but the carnival and mummer's plays.

Boo Radley is a figure in both the earlier Radley dramas, in which he is a character played by Jem, and in the Halloween drama, in which he participates actively. In both dramas, Boo Radley is a king- or father-killer, in the first instance of his own father, whom he attacks with scissors, and in the second instance of Mayella's father, whom he stabs with a knife. Ironically, on Halloween night, by killing Mayella's twisted father, he takes on the role of the good father protector of the Finch children.

It is not until the end of the novel, after Boo has rescued the children from Bob Ewell, that the children come face to face with the Other that has dominated their lives during these years of self-discovery. What once was regarded as a monster is now a known friend who pats Jem on the head and asks Scout to take him home.

Yet even from the first, when Boo is most terrifying, he is not an alien totally removed from their lives: Boo is closer to them than they first suspect. He is from the first metaphorically kin to them, a part of them even before he enters their minds and imaginations, and he has lived on the street with them for as long as they can remember. He is always there, near them, in a house that at one time was white and not unlike their own. In befriending Boo, the children are confronting a hidden part of themselves.

BLACK CHARACTERS AS OTHER

But the Other emerges in multiple guises in the course of the novel. For example, it is represented in the black people the children encounter, who are at the same time an integral part of their lives, yet totally separate, unknown, dark, mysterious. A black man's story dominates the second half of the novel, and the black church and Calpurnia, their housekeeper and surrogate mother, set up the theme of the black as the Other. Ironically, it is not until Scout and Jem attend church with Calpurnia that a sense of Calpurnia's difference reaches Scout. So egocentric is Scout's world, that it is not until that time that she realizes that Calpurnia is a person apart—has a life apart—from the Finch household. And Calpurnia doesn't seem to regard the white children as other than her own, almost as if she has two selves—one at her home, which is unknown to them, and one at the Finch house. Though in her mind and in that of the community her separateness, her blackness, is not entirely erased, for when she sleeps at the Finch's house while Atticus is gone, it is on a cot in the kitchen.

It is Calpurnia's idea to take the children to church with her, because she sees them as her children. She scrubs them with extra care and gives their clothes special attention: "'I don't want anybody sayin' I don't look after my children,' she muttered" (*TKM*, 118).

The church itself serves to point out the differences between blacks and whites. In the church's cemetery, during dry spells, the bodies are kept under ice cubes until the soil is workable enough to bury them. Instead of tombstones, broken glass and lightning rods and candles adorn the graves. In the church, the children are struck by the absence of "familiar ecclesiastical impedimenta" and hymnals, the references in the sermons to specific individual sinners, and especially, the "lining" of the hymns, whereby Zeebo sings a line and the congregation repeats it. They are also astounded to hear the minister order the doors locked to prevent anyone from leaving until ten dollars has been collected for the Robinson family.

Scout begins to see in Calpurnia's confrontation with another black woman, Lula, that there is some part of her lifelong caretaker of which she has never been aware:

> "What you want, Lula?" she asked, in tones I had never heard her use. She spoke quietly, contemptuously.
>
> "I wants to know why you bringin' white chillun to nigger church."
>
> "They's my comp'ny," said Calpurnia. Again I thought her voice strange: she was talking like the rest of them. (*TKM*, 119)

After they return from church, Jem also comments that though Calpurnia doesn't ordinarily talk like other black folks, she "talked like they did in church" (*TKM*, 125). At this point, Calpurnia's difference impresses itself on Scout: "That Calpurnia led a modest double life never dawned on me. The idea that she had a separate existence outside our household was a novel one, to say nothing of her having command of two languages" (*TKM*, 125). And in that moment when Scout senses Calpurnia's Otherness, she is attracted to her and wants to know more about her:

> "Cal, can I come to see you sometimes?"
>
> She looked down at me. "See me, honey? You see me every day."

"Out to your house," I said. "Sometimes after work? Atticus can get me."

"Any time you want to," she said. "We'd be glad to have you."
(*TKM*, 126)

Scout continues to ask Atticus to allow her to visit Calpurnia, but Aunt Alexandra, fiercely defending the white, Anglo-Saxon, southern genteel world against incursions from people unlike herself, stands between Scout and plans to investigate that dark and different life that Calpurnia lives. Understandably, it is Calpurnia, outcast as a black woman, who can sympathize with Boo, seeing his father, who has imprisoned him, as "the meanest man ever God blew breath into" (*TKM*, 12). In another sympathetic alliance between the self and the Other, the Finch children's sitting with the black people in the court-room balcony is emblematic of a common bond of mind and heart so at variance with most of the other white people in the building during the trial.

Curiously enough, Aunt Alexandra and her missionary society friends are also drawn to the "sin and squalor" of a dark Other—the poor Mrundas, who live a safe distance away and can be a subject of morbid fascination and pity, but who pose no threat to the ladies' comfortable view of their own white purity. Their prurience is illustrated in their fascination with the Mrundas' puberty rituals, their bark-chewing-induced psychedelic states, their having "no sense of family," and their practice of "putting the women out in the huts when their time came," a topic that mesmerizes them throughout their meeting (*TKM*, 228–31).

The attraction to the dark differences that Mayella Ewell sees in Tom Robinson leads to the rape trial. Tom's testimony reveals that she had called him into her yard repeatedly to do chores, finally luring him into the house: "'She'd call me in, suh. Seemed like everytime I passed by yonder she'd have some little somethin' for me to do.'" For Mayella, like the missionary ladies, the attraction of the Other is sexual: "'She reached up an' kissed me 'side of th' face'" (*TKM*, 194).

The theme of black people as the dark and compelling unknown is amplified by the introduction into the narrative of Dolphus Raymond, a white man who embraces the Other in taking a black wife and fathering her children. His choice to enter the separate world of the black woman heightens his own exotic character as, in the hearts of the community, he takes on the aura of the dark unknown. Before the trial, the children accord him and his mixed-race children the same spellbound attention that they had given Boo Radley. Dill, as insatiably curious about seeing a white man sitting with black men and women as he had been about Boo, has his questions answered by Jem:

> "Why's he sittin' with the colored folks?"
>
> "Always does. He likes 'em better'n he likes us, I reckon. Lives by himself way down near the county line. He's got a colored woman and all sorts of mixed chillun. Show you some of 'em if we see 'em.". . .
>
> "Jem," I asked, "what's a mixed child?"
>
> "Half white, half colored. You've seen 'em, Scout. You know that red-kinky-headed one that delivers for the drugstore. He's half white. They're real sad."
>
> "Sad, how come?"
>
> "They don't belong anywhere. Colored folks won't have 'em because they're half white; white folks won't have 'em because they're colored, so they're just in-betweens, don't belong anywhere." (*TKM*, 161)

Scout and Dill also come to be on friendly terms with the strange Dolphus Raymond, but as they first approach him, Scout especially is apprehensive. When Dolphus offers Dill a drink from his sack, reputed to hold whiskey in a Coca-cola bottle, she believes he is an "evil man" who is "evidently taking delight in corrupting a child." But for all their caution, it is his very depravity that attracts the children: "I had a feeling that I shouldn't be here listening to this sinful man who had mixed children and didn't care who knew it, but he was fascinating" (*TKM*, 201). They also are allowed into the secrets of this man, whom the community regards as darkly evil, when they find that his mystique is self-cultivated: the liquid he drinks from the bottle in his sack is really Coca-cola; he pretends it is whiskey to give the townspeople a reason they can accept for his living with black people. Further, when Dill and Scout approach him in the middle of the trial, they find him to be not an "evil man," but a gentle man who empathizes with Dill's inability to stomach the way Tom Robinson is treated in the courtroom: "You aren't thin-hided, it just makes you sick, doesn't it. . . .Things haven't caught up with that one's instinct yet" (*TKM*, 201).

SURROUNDED BY OTHERS

In the narrator's comparison of Mayella Ewell to Boo Radley and the mixed-race children of Dolphus Raymond, the reader understands that Mayella, the accuser of Tom Robinson, is an inversion of Scout, and also partakes of the dark and sexual world of the Other. Like Boo and the mixed-race children, she is utterly lonely and without a real place in the world:

> As Tom Robinson gave his testimony, it came to me that Mayella Ewell must have been the loneliest person in the world. She was even lonelier than Boo Radley, who had not been out of the house in twenty-five years. When Atticus asked had she any friends, she seemed not to know what he meant, then she thought he was making fun of her. She was as sad, I thought, as what Jem called a mixed child: white people wouldn't have anything to do with her because she lived among pigs; Negroes wouldn't have anything to do with her because she was white. She couldn't live like Mr. Dolphus Raymond, who preferred the company of Negroes, because she didn't own a riverbank and she wasn't from a fine old family. (*TKM*, 191–92)

Just as there is a connection between Boo and Tom and Mayella and the "mixed children," as well as a bond between the three children sitting in the balcony and the black people who surround them there, there is also a physical similarity joining Jem and Tom Robinson, the man for whom Jem mourns throughout the summer and fall: After

Ewell's attack on Jem, his left arm, like Tom Robinson's left arm, will carry the marks of a wound.

The encounter with the Other takes a ghastly and repulsive turn for the two Finch children, and especially for Jem, in their forced visits to Mrs. Dubose, an old sick woman who, they learn later, is addicted to morphine. Mrs. Dubose's role in the novel as a frightening character, very much like a witch, is established in the narrator's observation that "Mrs. Dubose was plain hell" (*TKM*, 6), and in Atticus's comparison of her house to the Radley house when Jem learns that he must enter it to read to her for a month.

Her gruesome appearance seals her, in Jem's words, as a "hell devil," and in entering her house, the children seem to be entering the devil's chambers. Their impression of her places her among those broomstick riders of the night, that fearful devil's company to which Boo Radley once belonged in the children's minds: "She was horrible. Her face was the color of a dirty pillowcase, and the corners of her mouth glistened with wet, which inched like a glacier down the deep grooves enclosing her chin. Old-age liver spots dotted her cheeks, and her pale eyes had black pinpoint pupils. Her hands were knobby, and the cuticles were grown up over her fingernails. Her bottom plate was not in, and her upper lip protruded; from time to time she would draw her nether lip to her upper plate and carry her chin with it. This made the wet move faster" (*TKM*, 106). As she is overtaken by morphine withdrawal, the children watch with unspeakable revulsion at the appalling witchlike transformation that resembles a Bosch painting:

> Something had happened to her. She lay on her back with the quilts up to her chin. Only her head and shoulders were visible. Her head moved slowly from side to side. From time to time she would open her mouth wide, and I could see her tongue undulate faintly. Cords of saliva would collect on her lips; she would draw them in, then open her mouth again. Her mouth seemed to have a private existence of its own. It worked separate and apart from the rest of her, out and in, like a clam hole at low tide. Occasionally it would say, "Pt," like some viscous substance coming to a boil. (*TKM*, 107)

The children's fascination even with this horror is attested to by Scout's voluntary accompaniment of Jem to the Dubose house. Atticus tells her, "You don't have to go with Jem you know" (*TKM*, 108).

It is through literature, myth, and art that the children make their first tentative approaches to the dark side of existence. By the time Dill arrives on the scene to awaken active interest in the dark side of life and the dark side of themselves, Jem has already read Bram Stoker's novel *Dracula*, but Dill brings the story a greater immediacy, not only through his experience of having seen, presumably, the Bella Lugosi film, but also through his active imagination. "Thus," the narrator reports, "we came to know Dill as a pocket Merlin, whose head teemed with eccentric plans, strange longings, and quaint fancies" (*TKM*, 8). Dill continually goes deeper into the life of the imagination, tempting them to come with him. Part of the reason for his enveloping creative viewpoint may come from the fact that Dill, through the eccentricity of his daily life, has already taken on certain shades of difference himself. Dill especially empathizes with Boo after he feels left out of his own "family"—he is miserable at home, then runs away, and wonders why Boo also never ran away (*TKM*, 144). The three children's common attraction to and literary experience with the vampire, and all the things outside of what they regard as the mundaneness of their lazy town experience, first draws them close together.

Another of their perennial favorites among literary works (which reinforces the reader's assumption that they are drawn to the extraordinary) is a series of "boy's books" with the hero Tom Swift. Their clear favorite is *The Gray Ghost*. The connection between these books and all that Boo Radley represents in their minds is made when Dill uses a trade of *The Gray Ghost* as a ploy to get Jem to make the first actual incursion into the dreaded Radley territory by running into their yard and touching the house. This book, one of the works that starts them on their quest toward knowledge of the Other, fittingly finds its way into the final scene of the novel, after Scout has held the hand of the monster and led him home. When she reenters her own home, Atticus, keeping watch at Jem's bedside, has picked up Jem's copy of *The Gray Ghost*, which has almost magically found its way into his hands. Realizing exactly what her father is reading certainly has a meaning for Scout on this evening, even if that meaning is an unintellectualized one:

> "Whatcha readin'?" I asked.
>
> Atticus turned the book over. "Something of Jem's. Called *The Gray Ghost*."
>
> I was suddenly awake. "Why'd you get that one?"
>
> "Honey, I don't know. Just picked it up." (*TKM*, 280)

As Atticus puts Scout to bed, she summarizes the Tom Swift tale for him, finding herself merging the fiction of one of their favorite books with their experience with Arthur Boo Radley and the inner and outer terrors with which they have become friendly:

> "Yeah, an' they all thought it was Stoner's Boy messin' up their clubhouse and throwin' ink all over it an'. . ."
>
> He guided me to bed and sat me down. He lifted my legs and put me under the cover.
>
> "An' they chased him'n' never could catch him 'cause they didn't know what he looked like, an' Atticus, when they finally saw him, why he hadn't done any of those things. . . Atticus, he was real nice. . . ."
>
> His hands were under my chin, pulling up the cover, tucking it around me.
>
> "Most people are, Scout, when you finally see them." (*TKM*, 281)

COURAGE

The children's encounters with difference comprise a kind of rite of passage, especially for Jem, who has reached puberty by the time of Tom Robinson's trial. And fundamental to their engagement with the Other is courage, one of many tokens of civilization in the novel. Courage seems to be defined in the novel as the intellectual mastery of the base fears of the flesh. The epitome of bravery is Atticus, the man who faces a mad dog in the streets and shoots it, the man who stops to chat with Mrs. Dubose ("It was at times like these when I thought my father, who hated guns and had never been to any wars, was the bravest man who ever lived." [*TKM*, 100]). Atticus is also the man who faces up to the racism in his community: In the first instance, he sits unarmed outside the jail where Tom Robinson is incarcerated, waiting for the armed lynch mob to arrive, and then encountering them head on; in the second instance, his courage is demonstrated in his open determination to give Tom Robinson the best defense he can muster in the face of fierce community opposition.

The children also have a lesson in courage from Mrs. Dubose, who has made up her mind that before she dies she will, by sheer force of will, and with only the enforced assistance of a child, free her body of the morphine to which she is addicted. Atticus tells the children: "I wanted you to see what real courage is, instead of getting the idea that courage is a man with a gun in his hand. . . . She was the bravest person I ever knew" (*TKM*, 112).

The children, in their steps toward coming to terms with reality by facing a frightening mystery, are also said to exhibit bravery. Jem is brave in touching the accursed Radley house, in trying to peep in the window of the house, and finally in attempting to retrieve his pants that got stuck on the wire fence when he was being shot at by Mr. Radley. It is a challenge to his bravery that provokes Jem into his first interaction with the Radley house. Dill accuses Jem of being too scared to run up and touch the house because people in Meridian, Mississippi weren't "such scary folks" as those in Maycomb. And Scout must summon up bravery in taking part in the Radley dramas since she knows, contrary to what Jem tells her, that Boo is alive; she has heard him laugh.

7

Legal Boundaries

The Gothic, as we have found, has to do with boundaries and walls of many kinds, those that lock people in and those that lock people out, those that protect and those that imprison, those that separate people behind walls of stereotyping and segregation and those that constantly threaten to crumble into chaos. *In To Kill a Mockingbird,* one system of barriers is constructed of two disjunctive legal codes: the codes people profess and those they choose to live by.

Atticus Finch's final hope in the defense of his black client accused of rape is that he may strike a favorable response in his summation to the south Alabama jury by invoking the official legal code of the United States:

> "There is one way in this country in which all men are created equal—there is one human institution that makes a pauper the equal of a Rockefeller, the stupid man the equal of an Einstein, and the ignorant man the equal of any college president. That institution, gentlemen, is a court. It can be the Supreme Court of the United States or the humblest J.P. court in the land, or this honorable court which you serve. Our courts have their faults, as does any human institution, but in this country of ours courts are

the great levelers, and in our courts all men are created equal."
(*TKM*, 205)

Atticus is grieved by what he cannot at this moment say, however: that the law of the land is one thing and "the secret court of men's hearts" quite another (*TKM*, 241). *TKM* presents the argument that the forces that motivate society are not consonant with the democratic ideals embedded in its legal system, and that the disjunction between the codes men and women profess and those they live by threatens to unravel individual lives as well as the social fabric. The setting of the novel was a time when rulings handed down from "the secret courts of men's hearts" became the laws they lived by openly, in defiance not only of all reason, but of the laws of the land they professed to uphold.

Laws and the legal system, both official and unofficial, form the skeleton of the narrative, a supposition suggested by the setting itself. Scout precociously reads the *Montgomery Advertiser*, the *Mobile Register*, and *Time* at a time when the national press was holding up for scrutiny the traditional breach in the South between the official system of legal justice and a contradictory, stronger tribal system. And in the summer of 1935, Atticus and Jem have an extended discussion about the composition of juries after the all-male, all-white jury convicts Tom Robinson of rape; all this occurs in the same year that the front page of the *Montgomery Advertiser* (April 4, 1935) explored the same issue, reporting that new trials had been ordered by the Supreme Court for two of the Scottsboro "boys" on the grounds that no blacks had served on their juries. The South's dual system of justice is freely acknowledged in the *Advertiser*'s editorial: blacks are not excluded from juries technically or legally, the editors claim, but "in common practice they are, of course."[1]

To Kill a Mockingbird, its title a reference to the shooting of a black man who makes a suicidal attempt to escape prison after being convicted of rape, is a study of legal boundaries in the broadest sense—boundaries of familial, communal, and regional codes, those of the drawing room and the school yard, those written and unwritten, and those that lie beneath the surface in dark contradiction of established law. Although its attorney hero, Atticus Finch, and the son that will follow in his footsteps, maintain a Christ-like goodness and wisdom in the memory of the narrator, what she unfolds in a story dependent on her father and brother is neither simple nor conclusive, for the laws and codes that drive these lives promote destruction as often as they keep it at bay.

Legalities of Plot

The trappings of plot and dialogue that direct the reader to the novel's complexity of legal barriers are numerous. *TKM* begins with a line from Charles Lamb, "Lawyers, I suppose, were children once," an inscription that refers to both children of Atticus Finch. The lines obviously refer to Jem who, the family understands, wants to be a lawyer like his father when he grows up, and who, as a child, is able to follow with greater interest and acumen than most adults the nuances of a trial that is the central event of the novel. Less obviously, the lines from Lamb refer to the daughter-narrator, who is taunted by the missionary ladies (because she attended the rape trial) for wanting to grow up to be a lawyer. The reader is not told if the narrator is a practicing attorney when she tells the story, but one does recognize her to be a student of the law in the broadest sense. The novel itself is, in part, her convincing brief for her father's sainthood, an ironic reversal of the usual novelistic cliché of adolescent (and Gothic) patricide. That Lee's readers, who are in a sense her jury, so readily and perpetually render a decision in Atticus's favor, closing the case, as it were, may in some way account for the silence of this authorial voice thereafter.

Relationships in the novel are often presented as legal boundaries. The cement of Maycomb, a community whose "primary reason for existence was government" (*TKM*, 131), is shown to be its formal and informal law: entailments (to which poor but honest Mr. Cunningham falls victim), compromises (between Scout and Atticus over her reading, for example), state legislative bills (introduced by Atticus, a legislator), treaties (between the Finch children and Miss Maudie over her azaleas), truancy laws (that the poor and lawless

Ewell children, but not Scout, are allowed to break), hunting and trapping laws (which are violated by Bob Ewell), and bending the law (an issue on which the novel closes). The pervasiveness of legal allusions extends even to Calpurnia, the Finch children's surrogate mother, who has been taught to read, and teaches her son to read, using Blackstone's *Commentaries*.

The major subplots arise from breaches of these legal boundaries: the arrest of the Finches' reclusive neighbor, Boo Radley, for disorderly conduct, and his later attack on his father; the children's trespassing on Radley property; the attempted lynching of Tom Robinson; the alleged rape of Mayella Ewell; and the assault and murder that conclude the novel.

The narrator frequently presents legalistic community relationships by negation, presenting both sympathetic and unsympathetic portraits of outlaws and outcasts, those outside certain traditional boundaries, who deliberately or inadvertently violate community codes. Of course, Scout is herself an outlaw, an observation that ladies in the area, especially Aunt Alexandra, have made from the moment Atticus is left alone to raise her and Jem with only the help of a black woman. Scout discovers her own oddity in first grade, when her teacher scolds her for having already learned to read. She drags home from school, "weary from the day's crimes" (*TKM*, 29), and from having repeatedly "been wallowing illicitly in the daily papers" (*TKM*, 17). Scout is understandably, immediately drawn to Dill, an outcast whose broken family scolds him for "not being a boy." Together, the three children, Scout, Jem, and Dill, are attracted to nightwalkers, outlaws in truth (Boo Radley) and fiction (Dracula).

In addition to the Radleys, other eccentric neighbors who influence the children's lives, because of their skirting of accepted codes of behavior in varying degrees, are Miss Maudie, who is railed at by footwashing Baptists for her luxurious azaleas (their blooms testimonies to her excessive love of the natural world), and Mrs. Dubose, a morphine addict. The trial also brings together victims and villains of both written and implicitly understood laws. Outside the courthouse, Scout is introduced to Dolphus Raymond, the man who has violated the southern code by preferring the company of blacks to whites, and has "got a colored woman and all sorts of mixed chillun" (*TKM*, 161). Tom Robinson broke a code that was silent but no less powerful, by feeling sorry for a white woman. Mayella Ewell violated an equally powerful unwritten code by kissing a black man. Of Mayella, Atticus says, "No code mattered to her before she broke it" (*TKM*, 204). The villainy of Mayella's father, Bob Ewell, arises from his unwillingness to be governed by any law, either internal or external: his crimes run from the petty violations of hunting and truancy laws to incest and attempted murder. His counterpart in lawless destruction and moral chaos on an international scale is Adolf Hitler, deplored by Scout's teacher Miss Gates, whom Scout has earlier overheard expressing her relief over the conviction of Tom Robinson, because she believes blacks have gotten too uppity.

Complexity of Social Codes

In several arenas, one might even say courtrooms, the characters of *TKM* play out a drama of legal and social codes, boundaries that are extraordinarily complex for such a tiny community. The primary ones, the Finch house, the courthouse, the schoolhouse, and the Ewell house, are little communities, each with its own scheme of relationships, each, like the community of Maycomb as a whole, with a hidden code as well as an open one. The codes here are based on physical difference as well as class: gender, race, and age. Most are instructed by a strong central presence.

The novel is a study of how Jem and Scout begin to perceive the complexity of social codes and how the configuration of relationships dictated by or set off by those codes fails or nurtures the inhabitants of these small worlds. In the aftermath of the court case, which is a moral victory and legal loss for their father, Jem and Scout discuss the heart of the matter, the fragmentation of the human community, one result of which is the mental classification of people in order, it seems, to make them less human. Neither Scout nor Jem can account for the boundaries they have begun to observe, society's division of people into hostile camps. Scout, never able to get a satisfactory answer from Aunt Alexandra, for whom differences have immense importance, speculates momentarily that these isolating distinctions have something to do with whether or not a group likes fiddle music and pot liquor. She rejects Jem's theory, at which he has arrived after long deliberation, that the key is literacy: " 'Naw, Jem, I think there's just one kind of folks. Folks'" (*TKM*, 227). Scout's magnanimity arises naturally from her experience as a child in the house of Atticus Finch, a household deceptively Edenic in its being unburdened with the barriers of complexity and duplicity that Jem and Scout will eventually discover in the real world. The children's maturation coincides with their exposure to the complex weave of codes in the social fabric of Maycomb. The children are first shaped by a home where love, truth, and wholeness have brought the household to a highly refined moral plane. As Tom Robinson's trial proceeds, the children become gradually aware of a world in sharp contrast to the one they have known. Bob Ewell is the antithesis of Atticus. As Ewell's realm surfaces, they become aware that perverse hidden codes and lawlessness, generally associated with the bigotry and ignorance in a place called Old Sarum, are manifest in the actions of the jury. Scout's suspicion of a dark underside of the community, first uncovered in the conviction of Tom, is alarmingly and unconsciously confirmed by Aunt Alexandra and the missionary society. In short, Old Sarum, the habitation of poor, hard-drinking dirt farmers on the edge of town, has invaded the boundaries around polite Maycomb.

Scout's realization of the difference between Maycomb's idealistic law and its unacknowledged but real laws begins in a setting where this disjunction had not previously existed, the Finch household, where the saintly Atticus, Christ-like in his code of honor, bestows a system of benevolent laws. The chief lesson he teaches his children is to try and walk around in the shoes of other people in order to understand them. He is a peacemaker, refusing to hunt or carry arms, insisting that his children turn the other cheek rather than resort to violence against human or beast. It is wrong, he tells Scout, even to hate Hitler. Atticus's saintliness has nothing to do with cowardice or impotence. He is a savior, capable of facing a mad dog and a lynch mob. Like

Christ, he is, Miss Maudie tells Jem, "born to do our unpleasant jobs for us" (*TKM*, 215). His brother, recognizing a Christ-like agony in Atticus's description of the impending trial, is lead to respond: "'Let this cup pass from you, eh?'" (*TKM*, 88). In explaining true courage to Jem and Scout, Atticus gives a general description of the tragic hero, which, as it turns out, is a description of his own role in the case of Tom Robinson: "It's when you know you're licked before you begin but you begin anyway and you see it through no matter what. You rarely win, but sometimes you do" (*TKM*, 112). Atticus's heroism is a quality that Maycomb's black population fully recognizes. In the most carefully crafted and emotionally packed moment of the novel, the one in which Atticus is leaving the courtroom after his defeat, Scout realizes that all the spectators in the balcony are standing, and she too is urged to her feet by the black preacher: "'Miss Jean Louise, stand up. Your father's passin'" (*TKM*, 211). (It is interesting to note that the word "passing" in the vocabulary of African-Americans refers both to the passage from life to eternal life and also from black to white identity, or vice versa.)

A house ordered by the laws of such a man might be expected to be as nurturing as it is eccentric. It is at one and the same time the most innocent and the most civilized of countries. Indeed, the Finch family seems to have moved upward through the various stages of civilization represented in the community. In their past is racial persecution (in the form of their slave-holding forebear), incest (which Atticus implies to Aunt Alexandra is the result of frequent intermarriage), and madness (Atticus's cousin Joshua St. Clair was institutionalized). While most of Maycomb is still in a primordial stage, the higher evolution of Atticus is apparent in his achievement of a refined moral code that rises above hate, egocentricity, and madness. Bigotry has been superseded by a higher law: people are to be regarded as individuals, human beings, not as dehumanized types. This is the crux of his argument at the trial: "'You know the truth, and the truth is this: some Negroes lie, some Negroes are immoral, some Negro men are not to be trusted around women—black or white. But this is a truth that applies to the human race and to no particular race of men'" (*TKM*, 204). And it is a position that he argues outside the courtroom as well. Of the lynch mob, he says, "'A mob's always made up o ‿ ‿ ple, no matter what. Mr. Cunningham was part of a mob last night, but he was still a man'" (*TKM*, 157).

CODES TO MAINTAIN BOUNDARIES

One of the keys to the benevolence of Atticus's law is that it blurs the lines that delineate gender and race, thus diminishing the artificial and superficial barriers that hamper and privilege. In the novel, the limitations of gender run parallel to the more obvious theme of the limitations of race. Scout, whose very nickname is boyish, is allowed to be herself—an adventurous tomboy. Even customs that recognize age are often disregarded: The children call Atticus by his first name, and Scout learns to read before she is "supposed" to. The same can be said of class barriers. Walter Cunningham, a poor Old Sarum child outside the Finch's social class, is invited home to lunch and treated as an honored guest. Scout, who is repulsed by Walter's failure to observe her own code of table behavior and says so, is severely scolded on this occasion for forgetting a more profound code of charity that is always observed in the Finch household. It is Calpurnia who chides her: "'Don't matter who they are, anybody sets foot in this house's yo' comp'ny, and don't you let me catch you remarkin' on their ways like you was so high and mighty'" (*TKM*, 24).

A higher, more civilized law is also seen in Atticus's rise above incestuousness and insularity, above parochialism and provincialism—in short, above self. By following Atticus's code, the children are taught to look and reach outward. Rising above self-protection and exclusion, they embrace difference.

Of all the societies that the children will ever encounter, their familial one is the most whole, and therefore, the most sane. Heart and head rule in harmony, inner and outer laws work in tandem, for there are no hidden agendas, no double standards, no dark secrets in their home. What Atticus has to say about race he will say in front of Calpurnia. When a child asks him something, he believes in answering truthfully. What Atticus preaches, he also practices: "'I can't live one way in town and another way in my home'" (*TKM*, 274). It is with this wholeness of spirit that Atticus confronts the madness of the town's society, just as he does a rabid dog in the street.

But Atticus's code is a far remove from the one maintained in Maycomb, Alabama, as Jem senses after Tom Robinson's conviction: "'It's like bein' a caterpillar in a cocoon, that's what it is,' he said. 'Like somethin' asleep wrapped up in a warm place. I always thought Maycomb folks were the best folks in the world, least that's what they seemed like'" (*TKM*, 215). The agents that destroy the children's Eden, in which benevolent laws are blind to artificial distinctions, are the citizens of Old Sarum and Bob Ewell, whose house is an inversion of Atticus's. Certain parallels invite the contrast: both Scout and Mayella Ewell are without biological mothers and without female friends. Scout never mentions another young girl her age at school or at play, and is even gradually being excluded from the companionship of Jem and Dill. Mayella does not even seem to understand the concept of friendship, male or female. This appears to make both girls more vulnerable, in that their fathers are consequently accorded more power for good or evil than they would have otherwise. Ewell and Atticus are pointedly opposite, however. Ewell hunts even out of season, but Atticus refuses to hunt at all. Ewell takes his children from school, while Atticus will not allow the dissatisfied Scout to be a truant. Ewell obviously beats Mayella viciously; Atticus has "never laid a hand" on his children (*TKM*, 88). Atticus is selfless in his love for Scout; Ewell is self-gratifying in his sexual abuse of Mayella. In sum, violence has been superseded in Atticus's life by love and laws; the violence of Ewell's life is untempered by law.

Jem, in particular, is traumatized by his experience in the dramatically different world of the courthouse. The law might have been sacred to Jem in theory, but he finds that in practice it is not. Here he encounters a mendacity, a mad doubleness that he has never experienced in his father's house. He discovers a powerful, concealed code at work, in complete contradiction to written law. The openly professed law, founded on a democratic ideal, is stated by Atticus in his summation at the trial: "'In this country our courts are the great levelers, and in our courts all men are created equal'" (*TKM*, 205). It is a sentiment repeated by Scout at school: Democracy, she parrots, means "'equal rights for all, special privileges for none'" (*TKM*, 245). However, even the apparatus of the court plainly countermands the official line. Only blacks are remanded by the court to Maycomb's jail. In the courtroom, black men and women are restricted to the balcony. No women and no blacks serve on juries. But more pernicious than any of these contradictions is the existence, as the narrator puts it, of "the secret court of men's hearts," where madness makes a mockery of equality before the law (*TKM*, 241). On the official level, Atticus had been appointed to defend Tom Robinson, but in the secret court of men's hearts, Atticus is faulted for doing the job that the community has given him.

Paralleling Jem's trauma in the male arena of the courthouse is Scout's enlightenment in the female arena. When Aunt Alexandra invades the Finch house in Maycomb, she brings with her a system of codification and segregation of the human family according to boundaries of class, race, and sex. Her codes delineate very narrowly ladies and gentlemen, black and white people, so-called good families and trash. Fearing contamination, she forbids Scout to visit Calpurnia's house or to invite Walter Cunningham to the Finch home again. Scout concludes that "Aunt Alexandra fitted into the world of Maycomb like a hand into a glove, but never into the world of Jem and me" (*TKM*, 131–32).

THE MISSIONARY SOCIETY

The larger society into which families, church, school, and local government fit is characterized by many of the Finches' neighbors and friends in general, and the missionary society in particular, all longtime residents who appear to be in the mainstream of the community. The perniciousness of this society arises from its system of dual contradictory codes: a hidden code, based on a rigid system of human categories, which contradicts an open and declared code. Superficially, the missionary ladies abide by the customs of gentility in "a world, where on its surface fragrant ladies rocked slowly, fanned gently, and drank cool water" (*TKM*, 233). They also, superficially, respond to the dictates of their religion by gathering together on errands of Christian charity. The official topic of discussion on this particular afternoon after Tom Robinson's trial is the remote Mrundas, a primitive African tribe infected with yaws and earworms, and, the ladies fear, possessed of no sense of family. Their expression of sympathy for the Mrundas is a charitable public formality declared in polite generalities. It is apparent, however, in a scene as primitive and tribal in its way as the Mrundas could ever be, that a code of greater countermanding force lies beneath the surface, one neither Christ-like nor charitable nor gentle, which undermines the external one they espouse. Regardless of what they profess, it is this dark code that actually governs their lives. They cuttingly and cruelly censor Atticus in his own house and in the presence of his nine-year-old daughter and his sister, their hostess. The missionary ladies can safely exclude black women from the sisterhood of the human race by failing to view them as other than types, establishing with heart and mind a segregation more pernicious than any system maintained by law. Mrs. Merryweather, the most prominent member of the society, who has devoted herself to bringing the word of Christ to the Mrundas, ironically speculates that trying to Christianize American black people may be useless. She and the other ladies are peevish and self-righteous in their plan to "convert" Tom Robinson's wife, regarding the black woman's membership in her own church as somewhat beside the point. They also grudgingly agree to "forgive" her for being the widow of a black man wrongfully convicted of raping a white woman. A corrective remark is provided by Scout, who, untrained in their racial distinctions, believes, before they name Helen Robinson, that the ladies are speaking of the white woman, Mayella Ewell, who lodged the accusation against Tom Robinson.

The meeting of the missionary society undercuts Atticus's and Miss Maudie's attempts to reassure the children that Maycomb isn't as bad as the members of the jury that convicted Tom Robinson. Atticus and Miss Maudie had maintained that the blind intolerance of the jury, which was made up of rural, uneducated, white males, does not characterize the larger community. The assurance given to Scout by the two adults she most respects in the world is shaken not only by the missionary society meeting, but by her teacher, Mrs. Evans, who also illustrates that geographical distance makes her propensities to democracy and charity eminently easier to maintain. Mrs. Evans flies the national colors by deploring Hitler's persecution of the Jews and by writing across the blackboard in large letters, "DEMOCRACY." But outside the courthouse after Tom Robinson's conviction, Scout glimpses a different set of rules by which the teacher lives, when she hears her assert that it was high time the blacks were taught a lesson for being too arrogant. What Scout feels but hasn't completely intellectualized yet is the same thing that is torturing Jem: Beneath the surface of the world they belong to and must live in lies another frightening force that threatens to unsettle it all. Just below the surface lie the poor Mrundas, Old Sarum, and Adolf Hitler.

VIOLENCE AND LAW

Harper Lee undoubtedly could write about her fiction what Nathaniel Hawthorne wrote of *The Scarlet Letter*—that the events of those years in which the work was conceived had a decided effect on the novel itself. The trial of Tom Robinson in *TKM*, a representation of an actual pattern of occurrences in Alabama during the late fifties, shows a jury made up of ignorant and bigoted rural Old Sarum southern males, because women and blacks were "in practice" excluded from juries, and educated middle- and upper-class whites refused to jeopardize their positions by serving on juries. Atticus clarifies: "Our stout Maycomb citizens aren't interested, in the first place. In the second place, they're afraid. . .Say, Mr. Link Deas had to decide the amount of damages to award, say Miss Maudie, when Miss Rachel ran over her with a car, Link wouldn't like the thought of losing either lady's business at his store, would he? So he tells Judge Taylor that he can't serve on the jury because he doesn't have anybody to keep the store while he's gone. So Judge Taylor excuses him" (*TKM*, 221).

The policy practiced by Martin Luther King, Jr., and his followers to counter violence with nonviolence was not as successful as

Atticus's nonviolent encounter with the Old Sarum lynch mob. In a similar real-life event, the wife of University of Alabama president O.C. Carmichael was pelted with eggs and stones when she appeared on the steps of her house to speak to a mob objecting to the admission to the university of Autherine Lucy, one instance in a series of events that showed "the apparent triumph of mob violence over the law of the land," as Suzanne Rau Wolfe notes in *The University of Alabama: A Pictorial History*.[2] Ironically, it is with reciprocal violence, perpetrated entirely outside the law in darkness, that the fictional children of a non-violent lawyer are saved. In short, in the dark hour of the novel, Atticus's higher law is an ineffective defense against Bob Ewell's chaos, as useless as facing a mad dog in the street without a gun. Only a miracle, some deus ex machina, in this case Boo Radley, can overcome chaos. Even a humane and civilized system of law becomes at some point and under certain circumstances severely limited when primitive, hidden codes or lawlessness emerge so powerfully. In the case of Boo Radley's killing of Bob Ewell, law is proven inadequate for another reason—specifically, that on occasion laws and boundaries must be overridden for justice to be done. Circumstance must temper honor; an individual human being's needs must supersede principle. Ewell's death must be reported as an accidental suicide instead of a homicide. It is not a situation that Atticus takes lightly: "If this thing's hushed up it'll be a simple denial to Jem of the way I've tried to raise him. . . .Jem and Scout know what happened. If they hear of me saying down town something different happened—Heck, I won't have them any more. I can't live one way in town and another way in my home" (*TKM*, 273).

But Atticus has always been more insistent that he and his own kind obey a higher law (which pulls them up the evolutionary ladder) than he expects the Ewells and Cunninghams to follow. Only when he finds that it is not Jem but Boo who has killed Bob Ewell does he relent to the secrecy that will circumvent a legal hearing. For Atticus knows Boo to be "one of the least of these," as Scripture delineates the earth's dispossessed, those who stand in for Christ. In a final act that secures Atticus's sainthood, he momentarily, hesitantly relinquishes for Boo Radley's sake what is most sacred to him: the code he lives by.

8

The Mockingbird's Song

The subject of *To Kill a Mockingbird* is also song, that is, expression: reading and literacy; both overt and covert attempts at articulation; and communicative art forms, including the novel itself. The particulars of setting in the novel are children's books, grade school texts, many different local newspapers and national news magazines, law books, a hymnal, and the reading aloud of Sir Walter Scott's *Ivanhoe*. Much of the novel's action is actually reading, for as the locals and the children believe, that is Atticus Finch's only activity. These expressions are not only attempts to have the self broadcast and realized; more significantly, they are attempts to establish connections beyond or through boundaries.

Contrary to the notion that language and art are cold (for example, the Dracula theme frequently expresses the cold tendency of artists to sacrifice everything, even their own humanity, for their art), in *TKM*, language and art are usually borne of love and linked to expressions of charity and affection. The Gothic degeneracy of *TKM* derives from love's opposite—imprisonment and insularity, producing, in the extreme, incest and insanity, a gazing in or a gazing back. Its opposite is the social self, which is civilized in its high and positive sense, and reaches out in the love that overcomes ego in language and art.

Language and other modes of communication are usually not only civilizing in a very positive way, but are avenues of benevolence, and even charity and love. In the novel, we remember Scout reading in Atticus's lap, Atticus reading as he keeps vigil beside Jem's bed, Atticus armed only with a book as he plans to protect Tom Robinson from a lynch mob. The society that imprisons Tom Robinson is the same one that imprisons Scout in the "Dewey Decimal System," Jem's garbled version of the pedagogical theories of the University of Chicago's father of progressive education, John Dewey, which are being faddishly inflicted on the children of Maycomb. The practical result of Dewey's system on Scout is to diminish or hinder her reading and writing, and along with it, her individuality. Each child is herded into a general category that determines whether he or she is "ready" to read or print or write ("We don't write in the first grade, we print" [*TKM*, 18]). The life of the mind and reading in particular is replaced in this progressive educational world with Group Dynamics, Good Citizenship, Units, Projects, and all manner of clichés. As Scout says, "I could not help receiving the impression that I was being cheated out of something. Out of what I knew not, yet I did not believe that twelve years of unrelieved boredom was exactly what the state had in mind for me" (*TKM*, 33).

As it is in a black man's account of slavery (*Narrative of the Life of Frederick Douglass*), reading and writing are major themes in *TKM*. Reading is first introduced with Dill's announcement that he can read, and Jem's counterboast that his sister, Scout, has been reading for years:

> "I'm Charles Baker Harris," he said. "I can read."
>
> "So what?" I said.
>
> "I just thought you'd like to know I can read. You got anything needs readin' I can do it. . . ." (*TKM*, 7)

The theme continues with Scout's difficulty with her first grade teacher, who resents that Scout is already able to read when she enters school. The heartfelt importance of reading to the child is considered as she contemplates its being denied to her. One notes in the following passage that reading is inextricably connected with her father and with the civilizing, everyday business of this world, that it is somehow as natural as breathing, and that she has learned that it is a crime in the view of her teacher, possibly because reading and writing (the latter taught to her by Calpurnia) are means of empowerment that place her beyond the control of her teacher:

> I mumbled that I was sorry and retired meditating upon my crime. I never deliberately learned to read, but somehow I had been wallowing illicitly in the daily papers. In the long hours of church— was it then I learned? I could not remember not being able to read hymns. Now that I was compelled to think about it, reading was something that just came to me, as learning to fasten the seat of my union suit without looking around, or achieving two bows from a snarl of shoelaces. I could not remember when the lines above Atticus's moving finger separated into words, but I had stared at them all the evenings in my memory, listening to the news of the day, Bills To Be Enacted into Laws, the diaries of Lorenzo Dow—anything Atticus happened to be reading when I crawled into his lap every night. Until I feared I would lose it, I never loved to read. One does not love breathing. (*TKM*, 17)

Atticus's civilizing power comes from his reading, a power he has taken on in place of the power of the gun. It is his sole pastime. The narrator reports, "He did not do the things our schoolmates' fathers did: he never went hunting, he did not play poker or fish or drink or smoke. He sat in the living room and read" (*TKM*, 89). Atticus is reading under the light outside the jail, with only a book and without a gun for protection, when the mob from Old Sarum arrives to harm his client, Tom Robinson. The novel closes with Atticus reading a book in Jem's room as he watches over his son. Members of The Idler's Club, the old men whose chief activity is attending court sessions together, know him as a lawyer whose skill arises from his being "'a deep reader, a mighty deep reader.'" They disparage his reluctance to depart from the civilizing force of the law by saying, "'He reads all right, that's all he does'" (*TKM*, 163). The love of reading is also true of Jem, for "no tutorial system devised by man could have stopped him from getting at books" (*TKM*, 32).

The theme of reading and writing as emblems for civilization are shown further in Jem's and Scout's discussion of what determines a "good" or "quality" or "old" family, and Scout's recognition of the importance of literacy: "'I think its how long your family's been readin' and writin'. Scout, I've studied this real hard and that's the only reason I can think of. Somewhere along when the Finches were in Egypt one of 'em must have learned a hieroglyphic or two and he taught his boy.'" To this Scout replies: "'Well, I'm glad he could, or who'da taught Atticus and them, and if Atticus couldn't read, you and me'd be in a fix'" (*TKM*, 226–27).

By contrast, the more powerless Old Sarum residents and black citizens of Maycomb County are rarely literate; they are generally able only to sign their names. Calpurnia is one of the few black people in the area who can read. She shocks the children with the information that only four members of her church can read, and one, whom she has taught to read, "lines" the hymns from the hymnbook for all the others to follow. And finally, in contemplating the meaning of "Old Families," Scout realizes that literacy has little to do with intelligence. What she doesn't realize is that it has a great deal to do with power of an intellectual sort.

While reading threads the narrative as surely as the subject of the law does, its meaning is less consistent and more elusive. Despite Scout's reservation about Jem's speculation that reading is connected to "Old Families," it is apparent that, in that it is connected to Atticus, reading denotes a pinnacle of civilized progress. The most civilized, the most humane, the wisest character is the one who reads obsessively.

The continuing powerlessness of the black and poor white people of Maycomb County is incidental to their inability to read, and their children, in contrast to Scout, are taken out of school, and thus denied their only access to power. A related idea is the control that Mrs. Dubose has over narcotics through forcing Jem to read to her. On the other hand, Zeebo, who leads the singing in the black church, is an example of one who imbues his reading with spirit and offers it as a gift to his people. Like Calpurnia, he has learned to read from Blackstone's *Commentaries*, but he uses the language he has been given from the cold letter of the law and imbues it with the warmth and life of the spirit, as he alone is able to lead his church congregation in singing hymns like "On Jordan's Stormy Banks." For the three children, reading, as we have seen, is a way of sharpening the imagination and gaining knowledge of the Other.

The children obsessively make attempts to communicate verbally with Arthur Radley, first by leaving a message for him in the tree, and then, in a blundering fashion, by sticking a note to his window.

Like other dispossessed people in the novel, Boo is doomed to communicate without language, though we suspect him to be literate, for he gives the children a spelling bee medal and is rumored to have stabbed his father in the leg while clipping articles from the newspaper. This begs the question of whether his assault on his father is provoked while he is reading the newspaper because it reminds him of his forced prohibition from establishing an intercourse with the world. So Boo attempts to reach out to the world through other means, and he is thwarted again. A real tragedy of Jem's boyhood, and most likely of Boo's life, is the severing of their channel of communication, the hole in the oak tree, which Boo's older brother cements up. The presents that he leaves in the tree appear to be Boo's last attempt to reach outside his prison. And each present, which is a means of communication, has significance. The chewing gum seems to be a way of proving that he isn't poisonous. The penny, an ancient medium of exchange, is something from the past. The spelling medal is also connected with literacy and communication. The carvings are works of art, communication, and love. The aborted mail profoundly affects Jem, who has played the part of Boo in the childhood dramas with conviction. Right after Jem's discovery of the cemented hole in the tree, Scout observes that "when we went in the house I saw he had been crying" (*TKM*, 63). For in shutting off Boo's avenue of expression, Mr. Radley, his brother, has thwarted Jem's as well, and has, more importantly, committed what would be a mortal sin in this novel—he has attempted to silence love.

Art forms other than literary ones occur in the novel, sometimes inadvertently communicating messages that the children don't intend.

There is the Radley drama, performed for their own edification, which the neighbors and Atticus finally see. And there is the snow sculpture of Mr. Avery, which the neighbors also recognize. Perhaps because these are self-serving art works, created without a sense of audience, as if art's communicative essence could be ignored, the effects of the play and the snow sculpture are not entirely charitable. On the other hand, Boo's art—the soap sculptures—are lovingly executed as a means of extending himself to the children.

Then there is the story the narrator tells, which, again, unites art with love, somehow making up for the novel's missed and indecipherable messages, like those so frequently found in the Gothic. The novel is a love story about, a love song to, Jem and Atticus, and to Dill, the unloved child, and Boo Radley, whose love was silenced.

The reader of the Gothic, according to William Patrick Day, is "essentially voyeuristic" (Day, 64). He further states, "Just as when we daydream and construct idle fantasies for ourselves, the encounter with the Gothic [as readers] is a moment in which the self defines its internal existence through the act of observing its fantasies" (Day, 65). Not only are characters in the Gothic enthralled, but the reader of the Gothic is as well. In the case of *TKM*, readers learn of the enthrallments of Jem, Dill, and Scout. But the reader of their story is also enthralled, not by the horror of racial mixing or the Dracularian Boo, but by the reminders of a lost innocence, of a time past, as unreal, in its way, as Transylvania. We, as readers, encounter the ghosts of ourselves, the children we once were, the simplicity of our lives in an earlier world. While the children's voyeurism is Gothic, our own as readers is romantic. In either case, the encounter is with the unreal. The children's encounter is in that underworld beneath reality, and ours is in a transcendent world above reality, which nostalgia and memory have altered. It is a world where children play in tree houses and swings and sip lemonade on hot summer days, and in the evenings, sit in their fathers' laps to read. Reality and illusion about the past is blurred. Within the novel's Gothicism and Romanticism, we as readers are enthralled with the past, and, like the responses elicited by the Gothic, we react with pain and pleasure to an involvement with our past world and our past selves.

Notes and References

1. Racial Climate in the Deep South

1. Harper Lee, *To Kill a Mockingbird* (New York: Warner Publications, 1982), 188; hereafter cited in the text.

2. Wayne Flynt, *Poor But Proud: Alabama's Poor Whites* (Tuscaloosa: University of Alabama Press, 1989), 281; hereafter cited in the text.

3. George Brown Tindall, *The Emergence of the New South, 1913–1945* (Baton Rouge: Louisiana State University Press, 1967), 354; hereafter cited in the text.

4. Virginia Hamilton, *Alabama: A Bicentennial History* (New York: W.W. Norton, 1977), 88; hereafter cited in the text.

5. Dan T. Carter, *Scottsboro: A Tragedy of the American South* (Baton Rouge: Louisiana State University Press, 1979), 115; hereafter cited in the text.

6. Virginia Foster Durr, *Outside the Magic Circle: The Autobiography of Virginia Foster Durr*, ed. Hollinger F. Barnard (Tuscaloosa: University of Alabama Press, 1985), 273–87.

7. Carl Grafton and Anne Permaloff, *Big Mules and Branchheads: James E. Folson and Political Power in Alabama* (Athens: University of Georgia Press, 1985), 197.

2. The Importance of *To Kill a Mockingbird*

1. Alice P. Hackett and James H. Burke, *Eighty Years of Best Sellers* (New York: R. R. Bowker, 1977), 25–75.

2. Arthur Applebee, *The Teaching of Literature in Programs with Reputations For Excellence in English* (Albany, New York: Center for the Study of Teaching and Learning of Literature, 1989), 10–25.

3. Richard Beach and James Marshall, *Teaching Literature in the*

Secondary Schools (New York: Harcourt Brace Jovanovich, 1991), 153.

4. *Survey of Lifetime Readers*, Prepared for the Library of Congress and Book-of-the-Month Club (Mansfield Center, Connecticut: Information Analysis Systems Corp., 1991), 1–8.

5. Jill P. May, "Censors as Critics: *To Kill a Mockingbird as a Case Study*," in *Cross-Culturalism in Children's Literature* (New York: Pace University Press, 1988), 91; hereafter cited in the text.

6. Edward Jenkinson, "Protecting Holden Caufield and His Friends," in *Teaching Secondary English: Reading and Applications*, ed. Daniel Sheridan (New York: Longman, 1993), 334–35.

7. Frank H. Lyell, "One-Taxi Town," *New York Times Book Review* (10 July 1960): 18.

8. "*To Kill a Mockingbird*," *Commonweal* (9 December 1960): 289.

9. Gary Wills, "From the Campaign Trail: Clinton's Hell-Raiser," *New Yorker* (October 1992): 93.

10. David Margolick, "Chipping at Atticus Finch's Pedestal," *New York Times* (28 February 1992): B1; hereafter cited in the text.

11. Claudia Carter, "Lawyers as Heroes: The Compassionate Activism of a Fictional Attorney Is a Model We Can Emulate," *Los Angeles Lawyer* (July-August 1988): 12. Matthew A. Hodel, "No Hollow Hearts," *American Bar Association Journal* (October 1991): 68–69.

13. Monroe Freedman, "Atticus Finch, Esq., R. I. P.," *Legal Times* (24 February 1992): 20.

14. R. Mason Barge, "Fictional Characters, Fictional Ethics," *Legal Times* (9 March 1992): 23.

15. Talbot D'Alemberte, "Remembering Atticus Finch's *Pro Bono* Legacy," *Legal Times* (6 April 1992): 26.

16. Timothy J. Dunn, "Atticus Finch *De Novo*: In Defense of Gentlemen," *New Jersey Law Journal* (27 April 1992): 15, 24.

17. Monroe Freedman, "Finch, the Lawyer Mythologized," *Legal Times* (18 May 1992): 25.

3. The Critical and Popular Reception

1. Granville Hicks, "Three at the Outset," *Saturday Review* (9 July 1960): 15; hereafter cited in the text.

2. Phoebe Adams, "Summmer Reading," *Atlantic* (26 August 1960): 98–99; hereafter cited in the text.

3. Malcolm Bradbury, "New Fiction," *Punch* (26 October 1960): 612; hereafter cited in the text.

Notes and References

4. Richard Sullivan, "Engrossing First Novel of Rare Excellence," *Chicago Sunday Tribune* (17 July 1960): 15; hereafter cited in the text.

5. "Sheer Purgatory," *New York Times Literary Supplement* (28 October 1960), 697.

6. Keith Waterhouse, "New Novels," *New Statesman* (15 October 1960): 580; hereafter cited in the text.

7. James B. McMillan, "*To Kill a Mockingbird*," *Alabama Review* (July 1961): 233.

8. Harding Lemay, "Children Play; Adults Betray," *New York Herald Tribune*, (10 July 1960): 5.

9. Herbert Mitgang, "Books of the Times," *New York Times* (13 July 1960): 33.

10. Katherine Gauss Jackson, "Books in Brief," *Harpers* (August 1960): 101; hereafter cited in the text.

11. Robert W. Henderson, "Lee, Harper: *To Kill a Mockingbird*," *School Library Journal* (15 May 1960): 44.

12. Phoebe Adams, "Summer Reading," *Atlantic* (26 August 1960): 98–99.

13. W. U. McDonald, Jr., "Harper Lee's College Writings," *American Notes and Queries* (May 1968): 131–32.

14. W. J. Stuckey, *The Pulitzer Prize Novels: A Critical Backward Look* (Norman: University of Oklahoma Press, 1981), 194.

15. William Going, "Store and Mockingbird: Two Pulitzer Novels about Alabama," in *Essays on Alabama Literature* (Tuscaloosa, Alabama: University of Alabama Press, 1975), 9–31.

16. Fred Erisman, "The Romantic Regionalism of Harper Lee," *Alabama Review* (1973): 122–36; Fred Erisman, "Literature and Place: Varieties of Regional Experience," *Journal of Regional Cultures* (Fall/Winter 1981): 144–53; R. A. Dave, "*To Kill a Mockingbird*: Harper Lee's Tragic Vision," in *Indian Studies in American Fiction*, ed. M. K. Naik (Kharwar: Karnatak University and The Macmillan Company of India, 1974): 311–23; Claudia D. Johnson, "The Secret Courts of Men's Hearts: Code and Law in Harper Lee's *To Kill a Mockingbird*," *Studies in American Fiction* (Autumn 1991): 129–39; hereafter cited in the text.

17. Thomas Shaffer, "Christian Lawyer Stories and American Legal Ethics," *Mercer Law Review* (Spring 1983): 879.

18. John D. Ayer, "Narrative in the Moral Theology of Tom Shaffer," *Journal of Legal Education* (March-June 1990): 173–93.

19. Timothy Hall, "Moral Character, the Practice of Law and Legal Education," *Mississippi Law Journal* (Winter 1990): 511–54.

5. The Gothic Tradition

1. David Punter, *The Literature of Terror: A History of Gothic Fictions from 1765 to the Present Day* (London: Longman, 1980), 1; hereafter cited in the text.

2. Kate Ferguson Ellis, *The Contested Castle: Gothic Novels and the Subversion of Domestic Ideology* (Urbana: University of Illinois Press, 1989); Maurice Levy, *Lovecraft: A Study in the Fantastic*, trans. S. T. Joshi (Detroit, Michigan: Wayne State University Press, 1988); hereafter cited in the text.

3. Eugenia C. DeLamotte, *Perils of the Night: A Feminist Study of Nineteenth-Century Gothic* (New York: Oxford University Press, 1990), xii; hereafter cited in the text.

4. William Patrick Day, *In the Circles of Fear and Desire: A Study of Gothic Fantasy.* (Chicago: University of Illinois Press, 1985), 411; hereafter cited in the text.

5. Irving Malin, *New American Gothic* (Carbondale: Southern Illinois University Press, 1962), 8; hereafter cited in the text.

6. The Danger and Delight of Difference

1. Ellie Ragland-Sullivan, *Jacques Lacan and the Philosophy of Psychoanalysis* (Urbana: University of Illinois Press, 1986), 15–16; hereafter cited in the text.

2. Annemarie De Waal Malefijt, *Religion and Culture* (New York: Macmillan, 1968); hereafter cited in the text.

3. D. W. Winnicott, *Playing and Reality* (New York: Basic Books, 1971), 54; hereafter cited in the text.

4. Rosemary Gould, *Child Studies through Fantasy* (New York: Quadrangle Books, 1972), 5; hereafter cited in the text.

5. Helen B. Schwartzman, *Transformations: The Anthropology of Children's Play* (New York: Plenum Press, 1986).

6. James Fraser, *The Golden Bough* (Chatham, New York: S. G. Phillips, 1959), 631.

7. Legal Boundaries

1. "The Supreme Court and Our Jury System," *Montgomery Advertiser* (April 2, 1935): 4.

2. Suzanne Rau Wolfe, *The University of Alabama: A Pictorial History* (Tuscaloosa: The University of Alabama Press, 1983), 201.

Bibliography

Primary Sources

Lee, Harper. *To Kill a Mockingbird*. New York: J. B. Lippincott, 1960.
    "Love—In Other Words." *Vogue*, 15 April 1961, 64–65.
    "Christmas to Me." *McCalls*, December 1961, 63.
    "A Word From Harper Lee." *The Screenplay of* To Kill a Mockingbird,
    by Horton Foote. New York: Harcourt Brace and World, 1964.
Capote, Truman. *The Grass Harp*. New York: Penguin Books, 1951.
    A Christmas Memory. New York: Random House, 1956.
    In Cold Blood. New York: Random House, 1965.
    The Thanksgiving Visitor. New York: Random House, 1967.
    ———. *Other Voices—Other Rooms*. New York: Random House, 1968.
Sergel, Christopher. *To Kill a Mockingbird*. Woodstock, Ill.: Dramatic
    Publishing Company, 1970.
To Kill a Mockingbird: A One-Act Play. Woodstock, Ill.: Dramatic Publishing
    Co., 1990.

Secondary Sources

Literary and Legal Commentary on *To Kill a Mockingbird*

Ayer, John D. "Narrative in the Moral Theology of Tom Shaffer." *Journal of*

Legal Education, March-June 1990, 173–93.

Barge, R. Mason. "Fictional Characters, Fictional Ethics." *Legal Times*, 9 March 1992, 23.

Carter, Claudia A. "Lawyers as Heroes: The Compassionate Activism of a Fictional Attorney Is a Model We Can Emulate." *Los Angeles Lawyer*, July-August 1988, 13.

Dave, R. A. "*To Kill a Mockingbird*: Harper Lee's Tragic Vision," in *Indian Studies in American Fiction*, edited by M. K. Naik. Dharwar: Karnatak University and The Macmillan Company of India, 1974.

D'Alemberte, Talbot. "Remembering Atticus Finch's *Pro Bono* Legacy." *Legal Times*, 6 April 1992, 26.

Dunn, Timothy. "Atticus Finch *De Novo*: In Defense of Gentlemen." *New Jersey Law Journal*, 27 April 1992, 15.

Erisman, Fred. "The Romantic Regionalism of Harper Lee." *Alabama Review*, 1973, 122–36.

———. "Literature and Place: Varieties of Regional Experience." *Journal of Regional Cultures*, Fall/Winter 1981, 144–53.

Freedman, Monroe. "Atticus Finch, Esq., R.I.P." *Legal Times*, 24 February 1992, 20.

———. "Finch: The Lawyer Mythologized." *Legal Times*, 18 May 1992, 25.

Going, William. "Store and Mockingbird: Two Pulitzer Novels about Alabama," in *Essays on Alabama Literature*. Tuscaloosa: University of Alabama Press, 1975.

Hall, Timothy L. "Moral Character, the Practice of Law, and Legal Education." *Mississippi Law Journal*, Winter 1990, 511–54.

Hodel, Matthew A. "No Hollow Hearts." *American Bar Association Journal*, October 1991, 68–69.

Johnson, Claudia D. "The Secret Courts of Men's Hearts: Code and Law in Harper Lee's *To Kill a Mockingbird*." *Studies in American Fiction*, Autumn 1991, 129–39.

Margolick, David. "Chipping at Atticus Finch's Pedestal." *New York Times*, 28 February 1992, B1.

McDonald, W. U. "Harper Lee's College Writings." *American Notes and Queries*, May 1968, 131–32.

Shaffer, Thomas L. "Christian Lawyer Stories and American Legal Ethics." *Mercer Law Review*, Spring 1982, 877–901.

Faith and the Professions. Salt Lake City, Utah: Brigham Young University Press, 1987.

"The Moral Theology of Atticus Finch." *University of Pittsburgh Law Review*, 1981, 197–204.

On Being a Christian and a Lawyer. Salt Lake City: Brigham Young

Bibliography

University Press, 1981.

Streitfeld, David. "Book Report." *Washington Post*, 8 December 1991, Book World section, 15.

Stuckey, W. J. *The Pulitzer Prize Novels: A Critical Backward Look.* Norman: University of Oklahoma Press, 1981.

Reviews

"About Life and Little Girls." *Time*, 1 August 1960, 70–71.

Adams, Phoebe. "Summer Reading." *Atlantic*, 26 August 1960, 98–99.

Bradbury, Malcolm. "New Fiction." *Punch*, 26 October 1960, 611–12.

Bruell, Edwin. "Keen Scalpel on Racial Ills." *English Journal*, December 1964, 660.

"Fiction: Three to Make Ready." *Kirkus Review*, 1 May 1960, 360.

Haselden, Elizabeth Lee. "We Aren't in It." *Christian Century*, 24 May 1961, 655.

Henderson, Robert W. "Lee, Harper. To Kill a Mockingbird." *School Library Journal*, 15 May 1960, 44.

Hicks, Granville. "Three at the Outset." *Saturday Review*, 23 July 1960, 15–16.

Jackson, Katherine Fauss. "Books in Brief." *Harpers*, August 1960, 101.

Lemay, Harding. "Children Play; Adults Betray." *New York Herald Tribune*, 10 July 1960, 5.

Lyell, Frank H. "One-Taxi Town." *New York Times Book Review*, 10 July 1960, 5, 18.

McMillan, James B. "*To Kill a Mockingbird.*" *Alabama Review*, July 1961, 233.

Mitgang, Herbert. "Books of the Times." *New York Times*, 13 July 1960, 33.

Schumach, Murray. "Prize for Novel Elates Film Pair." *New York Times*, 19 May 1961, 26.

"Sheer Purgatory." *Times Literary Supplement*, 28 October 1960, 697.

Sullivan, Richard. "Engrossing First Novel of Rare Excellence." *Chicago Sunday Tribune*, 17 July 1960, 15.

"*To Kill a Mockingbird.*" *Commonweal*, 9 December 1960, 289.

"*To Kill a Mockingbird.*" *New Yorker*, 10 September 1960, 203–4.

Waterhouse, Keith. "New Novels." *New Statesman*, 15 October 1960, 580.

Works about Readership and Censorship

Applebee, Arthur. *The Teaching of Literature in Programs with Reputations for Excellence in English.* Albany, New York: Center for the Study of Teaching and Learning of Literature, 1989.

A Study of Book-Length Works Taught in High School English Courses. Albany, New York: Center for the Study of Teaching and Learning of Literature, 1989.

Beach, Richard and James Marshall. *Teaching Literature in the Secondary Schools.* New York: Harcourt Brace Jovanovich, 1991.

Davis, James and Hazel Davis, eds. *Your Reading: A Booklist for Junior High and Middle School Students.* Urbana, Ill.: National Council of Teachers of English, 1988.

Hacket, Alice P. and James H. Burke. *Eighty Years of Best Sellers: 1875–1975.* New York: R. R. Bowker, 1977.

Jenkinson, Edward. "Protecting Holden Caufield and His Friends from the Censors," in *Teaching Secondary English: Readings and Applications,* edited by Daniel Sheridan. New York: Longman, 1993.

Maxwell, Rhoda J. and Mary Jordan Meiser. *Teaching English in Middle and Secondary Schools.* New York: Macmillan, 1992.

May, Jill P. "Censors as Critics: *To Kill a Mockingbird* as a Case Study," in *Cross-Culturalism in Children's Literature: Selected Papers from the Children's Literature Association.* New York: Pace University Press, 1988.

Survey of Lifetime Readers. Prepared for the Library of Congress and Book of the Month Club. Mansfield Center, Connecticut: Information Analysis Systems Corp., 1991.

Biographical References

Altman, Dorothy Jewell. "Lee, Harper," in *Dictionary of Literary Biography: American Novelists since World War II,* edited by James E. Kibler, Jr. Detroit: Gale Research, 1980.

Blackwell, Louise. "Harper Lee," in *Southern Writers: A Biographical Dictionary,* edited by Joseph Flora and Louis Rubin. Baton Rouge: Louisiana State University Press, 1979.

Clarke, Gerald. *Capote.* New York: Simon and Schuster, 1988.

Inge, M. Thomas. *Truman Capote: Conversations.* Jackson: University Press of Mississippi, 1987.

"Lee, (Nelle) Harper," in *Contemporary Authors,* edited by Clare D. Kinsman. Detroit: Gale Research, 1975.

"Lee, (Nelle) Harper," in *Contemporary Literary Criticism,* edited by Roger Matuz. Detroit: Gale Research, 1990.

"Lee, (Nelle) Harper," in *Current Biography,* edited by Charles Moritz. New York: H. W. Wilson, 1961.

Works on the Gothic, Terror, and Dracula

Carringer, Robert L. "Poe's Tales: The Circumscription of Space," in *The Tales*

Bibliography

of Poe, edited by Harold Bloom. New York: Chelsea House, 1987.

Day, William Patrick. *In the Circles of Fear and Desire: A Study of Gothic Fantasy.* Chicago: University of Chicago Press, 1985.

DeLamotte, Eugenia C. *Perils of the Night: A Feminist Study of Nineteenth-Century Gothic.* New York: Oxford University Press, 1990.

Ellis, Kate Ferguson. *The Contested Castle: Gothic Novels and the Subversion of Domestic Ideology.* Urbana: University of Illinois Press, 1989.

Fiedler, Leslie. *Love and Death in the American Novel.* New York: Stein and Day, 1960.

Freud, Sigmund. "The 'Uncanny,'" in vol. 17, *Standard Edition of the Complete Works of Sigmund Freud,* translated by James Strachey. London: Hogarth Press, 1955.

Heller, Terry. *The Delights of Terror: An Aesthetics of the Tale of Terror.* Urbana: University of Illinois Press, 1987.

Jackson, Rosemary. *Fantasy.* New York: Methuen, 1981.

Kennedy, J. Gerald. "Phantasms of Death in Poe's Fiction," in *The Tales of Poe,* edited by Harold Bloom. New York: Chelsea House, 1987.

Malin, Irving. *New American Gothic.* Carbondale: Southern Illinois University Press, 1962.

Punter, David. *The Literature of Terror: A History of Gothic Fictions from 1765 to the Present Day.* London: Longman, 1980.

Ragland-Sullivan, Ellie. *Jacques Lacan and the Philosophy of Psychoanalysis.* Urbana: University of Illinois Press, 1986.

Sedgwick, Eve. *The Coherence of Gothic Conventions.* New York: Arno Press, 1980.

Thompson, G.R. *Poe's Fiction: Romantic Irony in the Gothic Tales.* Madison: University of Wisconsin Press, 1973.

Twitchell, James. B. *The Living Dead: A Study of the Vampire in Romantic Literature.* Durham, N.C.: Duke University Press, 1981.

Weiskel, Thomas. *The Romantic Sublime.* Baltimore: Johns Hopkins University Press, 1976.

Works on Play and Ritual

Frazer, James George. *The New Golden Bough.* Chatham, New York: S. G. Phillips, 1959.

Gould, Rosemary. *Child Studies through Fantasy.* New York: Quadrangle Books, 1972.

Malefijt, Annemarie De Waal. *Religion and Culture.* New York: Macmillan, 1968.

Schwartzman, Helen B. *Transformations: The Anthropology of Children's Play.* New York: Plenum Press, 1978.

Turner, Victor. *From Ritual to Theatre*. New York: Performing Arts Journal Publication, 1982.

Winnicott, D.W. *Playing and Reality*. New York: Basic Books, 1971.

Historical Sources

Carter, Dan T. *Scottsboro: A Tragedy of the American South*. Baton Rouge: Louisiana State University Press, 1979.

Cash, W. J. *The Mind of the South*. New York: Vintage Books, 1969.

Crenshaw, Miles and Kenneth A. Miller. *Scottsboro: The Firebrand of Communism*. Montgomery, Ala.: Press of the Brown Printing Company, 1936.

Durr, Virginia Foster. *Outside the Magic Circle: The Autobiography of Virginia Foster Durr*, edited by Hollinger F. Barnard. Tuscaloosa: University of Alabama Press, 1985.

Flynt, Wayne. *Poor But Proud: Alabama's Poor Whites*. Tuscaloosa: University of Alabama Press, 1989.

Friedman, Leon, ed. *Southern Justice*. New York: World Publishing, 1963.

Grafton, Carl and Anne Permaloff. *Big Mules and Branchheads: James E. Folson and Political Power in Alabama*. Athens: University of Georgia Press, 1985.

Hackney, Sheldon. *Populism to Progressivism in Alabama*. New Jersey: Princeton University Press, 1969.

Hamilton, Virginia Van der Veer. *Alabama: A Bicentennial History*. New York: W. W. Norton, 1977.

Kluger, Richard. *Simple Justice: The History of* Brown v. Board of Education *and Black America's Struggle for Equality*. New York: Vintage Books, 1977.

National Association for the Advancement of Colored People, The. *Thirty Years of Lynching: 1889–1919*. New York: Arno Press and the New York Times, 1969.

Peltason, J.W. *Fifty-Eight Lonely Men: Southern Federal Judges and School Desegregation*. Urbana: University of Illinois Press, 1971.

Raines, Howell. *My Soul is Rested: Movement Days in the Deep South Remembered*. New York: G.P. Putnam's Sons, 1977.

Tindall, George Brown. *The Emergence of the New South, 1913–1945*. Baton Rouge: Louisiana State University Press, 1967.

Wiener, Jonathan M. *Social Origins of the New South: Alabama, 1860–1885*. Baton Rouge: Louisiana State University Press, 1978.

Wills, Gary. "From the Campaign Trail: Clinton's Hell-Raiser." *New Yorker*, October 1992, 93.

Index

The Author

Claudia Durst Johnson has for 20 years been a professor, and, for 12 years, chair of the Department of English at the University of Alabama in Tuscaloosa. Professor Johnson is the author of a book on Nathaniel Hawthorne, *The Productive Tension of Hawthorne's Art* (1981), and a book on nineteenth-century America, *American Actress: Perspective on the Nineteenth Century* (1984). She is also the coauthor, with Henry E. Jacobs, of *An Annotated Bibliography of Shakespearean Burlesques, Parodies, and Travesties* (1976), and, with Vernon E. Johnson, of *Nineteenth-Century Theatrical Memoirs* (1982). Her articles on literature and theater have appeared in *American Literature*, *American Quarterly*, *Studies in American Fiction*, *New England Quarterly*, *Nineteenth-Century Theatre Research*, *American Literary Scholarship*, *Transcendental Quarterly*, and the *Columbia Literary History of the United States*, and in collections published by Crown Publishers and the University Presses of Duke, Illinois, Massachusetts, Alabama, and Pennsylvania.